MW01116266

THE BODYBUILDING MEAL PREP

Guide & Cookbook

Learn How to Boost Your Muscle Growth and Burn Fat with these Easy&Fast, Make-Ahead, High-Protein, and Macro-Friendly Recipes for a Shredded Body

Harold D. Mitchell

CONTENTS

HIGH PROTEIN MAIN COURSES 68

HIGH PROTEIN DESSERTS 95

© Copyright 2023 - All rights reserved.

The content contained within this book may not be reproduced, duplicated or transmitted without direct written permission from the author or the publisher.

Under no circumstances will any blame or legal responsibility be held against the publisher, or author, for any damages, reparation, or monetary loss due to the information contained within this book, either directly or indirectly.

Legal Notice:

This book is copyright protected. It is only for personal use. You cannot amend, distribute, sell, use, quote or paraphrase any part, or the content within this book, without the consent of the author or publisher.

Disclaimer Notice:

Please note the information contained within this document is for educational and entertainment purposes only. All effort has been executed to present accurate, up to date, reliable, complete information. No warranties of any kind are declared or implied. Readers acknowledge that the author is not engaged in the rendering of legal, financial, medical or professional advice. The content within this book has been derived from various sources. Please consult a licensed professional before attempting any techniques outlined in this book.

By reading this document, the reader agrees that under no circumstances is the author responsible for any losses, direct or indirect, that are incurred as a result of the use of the information contained within this document, including, but not limited to, errors, omissions, or inaccuracies.

Introduction

When we think of bodybuilding, the first thing that comes to mind is going to the gym and lifting weights. We might also think of hiring a personal trainer and buying protein powders in bulk. While this is not completely incorrect, there are other aspects to bodybuilding that require a little more understanding in general, from dietary changes and adding or eliminating certain foods to making small changes to our already very busy lifestyles.

Making the decision to change your lifestyle for the better is one huge step, and it is certainly encouraging and a positive feature to add to one's life. One of the biggest changes we can make is to change our diets and eating habits, and once we decide what we want the end results to be, the fun begins. Some people change their dietary requirements either to lose weight or to build up muscle, and oftentimes both. In order to reach our goals, we need to take a look and study meal options and the importance of healthy foods, which go hand-in-hand with enhancing our overall health and lifestyle changes. A good place to start is to try and eat more seasonal foods if available at any given time. Changing our diets is not limited to seasons, but there are benefits.

Eating seasonal vegetables and fruits is a sustainable method of changing your diet, and it includes some health benefits. Not only does it encourage a person to eat only produce that is available in its respective season, it also helps the natural cycle of life of that produce by letting the environment use its natural resources, and in season produce is much more flavorful and nutritious. Seasonal eating may also include eating certain other food items, such as meat or fish, during a particular part of the year.

Storing food correctly allows the food to be eaten over a period of time (generally weeks to months) after the seasonal harvest rather than immediately. Food storage, preservation, and transport, including delivery to consumers, are important to the security of food, especially for people all over the world who must rely on other people to produce their food.

Storing food correctly plays an important role in meal preparation. Most foods can be frozen and thawed for reuse later with very low risk of bacteria and mold buildup, making this option the best viable way to save any leftovers that will be useful at a later time. Using the correct storing materials extends the quality of food for longer, even though some food items may lose some flavor. A properly working fridge and freezer is required in these cases, but there are also some dos and don'ts when we store food for long periods of time as well. We can also benefit from knowing which foods can and cannot be stored in the freezer and how to store them.

When we prepare meals for later use and if we are preparing them for specific dietary purposes, we need to learn some important information such as nutritional value in order to work out a well-balanced diet.

In the first chapters we list various foods and the quantity of their nutritional values in specific volumes to give us a good idea of what we are doing and what we are looking for. It is also helpful to know how to work out sufficient health requirements according to our own individual bodies' needs by using our overall build, such as our weight, to configure what we need in order to reach our dietary requirements and goals.

Preparing meals and planning ahead does not only pertain to gaining body mass, but is also essential when we want to lose weight or simply eat healthier. The point is that there are many reasons and benefits to planning and preparing meals in advance. It is also a great way to learn new methods of cooking, try our new recipes and experiment with the foods we love, and get reacquainted with foods we may not be too fond of.

Let this book be the first step into the flavorful and colorful world of food and the beginning of a better, healthier lifestyle so that we can win our energy and brain power back.

Why Make Meal Prep?

Changing one's entire lifestyle and diet into something new can be very challenging because we need to learn to form new and better habits while eradicating old bad ones. Whether we want to lose weight or gain muscle mass, a change in diet is key, and what works the best is when we plan ahead and prepare our meals in advance. Not only will meal prep save you from spending unnecessary amounts of money on takeout in a hurry, it will also help you stick to a meal plan and reap all the nutritional and health benefits as a whole. Meal prep also teaches you to consider creating more balanced meal plans so that you do not skip on essential nutrients.

Understanding the functions of important and essential nutritional value of food items makes it simpler to work out a meal plan knowing your body is receiving all the value it can possibly get out of your diet. The body needs certain amounts of protein, carbohydrates, fats, and other supplements to function at its best, and each of these elements play an important yet different role in the upkeep of our bodies. Our bodies use what we call macronutrients, which are broken down into smaller parts during digestion and as such are used for producing energy, building muscle, and cell structuring.

Carbohydrates

Carbohydrates are broken down into sugar molecules, better known as glucose. Keep in mind that this rule does not apply to dietary fiber, which simply passes through our systems undigested; however, some fibers do get fermented in our colons by bacteria.

These are the main functions of carbohydrates:

•   Glucose is the body's preferred source of energy for red blood cells, the brain, and the central nervous system. Carbs provide instant energy.

•   The fiber in carbs promotes healthy bowel movements.

•   Fiber fills us up while eating, which means we eat less and feel fuller for much longer periods of time.

•   Glucose is stored as glycogen in the liver and muscles for future use should you need more energy, such as after an extended period of fasting.

Proteins

Proteins are what is digested into amino acids. There are 20 amino acids with very important functions for the body, nine of which must be obtained from food sources and are very essential.

These are the main functions of amino acids in proteins:

•   They help create new protein within our bodies and are used to repair and build muscle and tissue.

- They also provide structure to our bodies' nails, organs, hair, skin, and cell membranes.

- Amino acids help to maintain the pH balances within our bodies.

- They also create new hormones and enzymes. The body cannot create these without the correct amino acids.

Fats

Glycerol is what happens when fats are broken down into fatty acids.

These are the functions of lipids and fats:

- Lipids are an essential component for cell membranes.

- Fats that are stored as energy serve as an energy reserve, which can be used in periods where we eat fewer calories than we need.

- Lipids also help to promote and transport the absorption of fat-soluble vitamins A, D, E, and K.

- Fat also protects and insulates organs.

With all the above-mentioned information, we can better understand the importance of certain foods and why we need to consume them. Even though we were taught as kids to eat our vegetables, and it is true, we still need to remember that there is a balance we need to keep, and too much of a good thing can also be a not-so-good thing.

Scientific Information

Macronutrients, also referred to as "macros," are nutrients our bodies need in large amounts in order to function properly and at their best. Protein, carbohydrates, and fat are the three main macros. These nutrients are essentials that our bodies cannot make or make enough of. Macros provide our bodies with energy, and needs are based really on personal circumstances; each macro also contains other nutrients essential to our health and bodies, each with their own purpose.

Proteins provide our bodies with amino acids, while fats contain important fatty acids. Calories are the body's main energy source. However, our bodies can use other sources of energy when needed. The calorie content of each of the macros are:

- Carbohydrates: 4 calories per 1 g

- Protein: 4 calories per 1 g

- Fat: 9 calories per 1 g

- Alcohol: 7 calories per 1 g

Alcohol is included here for those who prefer an alcoholic beverage from time to time. Below are a list of sources for each of the macros:

Carbohydrates

- Whole grains: brown rice, farro, barley

- Vegetables: corn, potatoes, peas, and other starchy vegetables

- Fruits: figs, bananas, apples, mangoes

- Legumes and beans: lentils, black beans, chickpeas

- Dairy products: yogurt, milk

Protein

- Eggs: egg whites in particular

- Seafood: cod, salmon, shrimp

- Poultry: turkey, chicken

- Red meat: lamb, beef, pork

- Dairy: cheese, yogurt, milk

- Seeds and nuts: pumpkin seeds, almonds

- Legumes and beans: lentils, black beans, chickpeas

- Soy products: edamame, tofu, tempeh

Fat

- Dairy products: cheese, full-fat yogurt

- Seeds and nuts: pumpkin seeds, almonds

- Fatty fish: herring, salmon

- Coconut: dried, fresh, coconut oil

- Extra virgin olive oil

- Avocados: fresh, avocado oil

Calculating Protein, Calorie Intake, and Portion Sizes According to Body Mass

In order to sustain ourselves and maintain healthy lifestyles, we can calculate these by using our body mass. This would include our height, weight, gender, and age to be taken into consideration for accurate calculations, and obviously for best results in accordance with our specific needs. Keep in mind that we need to also consider our goals, daily activity, and overall fitness in order to be successful in this specific task.

While it is easy to look up this function on the internet, it is handy to have a summarized explanation at hand to refer to when required. Tracking our macro intake really covers our intake of carbohydrates, fats, and protein very well and helps in our meal planning and portion sizes. This would generally be referred to as our macronutrient ratio.

If we do not have any scientific knowledge or tools to auto-calculate our intake, we make use of the hand system, and it works very well. Here is how it works:

Protein such as eggs: Our own palmfuls of protein foods are the most accurate portions of protein intake at a time.

Vegetables: The amount of vegetables as the size of our fists is sufficient.

Carbohydrates such as pastas: When we cup our hands and portion this amount of carbs we will not be overdoing it in one sitting.

Fat: Our fat intake at a time should not be more than the amount we can measure with our thumbs.

Foods With High Protein Content

Foods with protein content are plenty, but a comprehensive list of foods will help you understand how to utilize them in your diet. Out of four food groups, the listed items will also tell you the protein content per measuring unit, respectively. They are:

High-Protein Eggs and Dairy

- Eggs: 6 g per 1 large egg

We often see oozes of eggs used in videos and articles for bodybuilding purposes, and there is a very good reason for this. Eggs are low in carbohydrates and filled with goodness because they contain omega-3 and branched-chain amino acids (BCAA). BCAAs are a combination of not two, but three very essential amino acids, namely leucine (1.079 g), isoleucine (0.0686 g), and valine (0.767 g). Eggs contain nine out of the 20 BCAAs.

- Greek yogurt: 23 g per 8 oz

- Cottage cheese: 148 g per half cup

- Swiss cheese: 8 g per oz

- Two percent milk: 8 g per cup

- Casein and whey protein powder: 24–30 g per scoop

- Ready-to-drink (RTD) protein drinks: 16–20 g per cup

- Frozen Greek yogurt: 6 g per half cup

High-Protein Seafood

- Light tuna: 22 g per 3 oz

- Yellowfin tuna: 25 g per 3 oz

- Halibut: 23 g per 3 oz

- Octopus: 25 g per 3 oz

- Sockeye salmon: 23 g per 3 oz

- Tilapia: 21 g per 3 oz

- Anchovies; 24 g per 3 oz

- Sardines: 21 g per 3 oz

High-Protein Meats

- Chicken breast: 23 g per 3 oz

- Ground beef: 18 g per 3 oz

- Pork chops: 26 g per 3 oz

- Turkey breast: 24 g per 3 oz

- Corned beef: 24 g per 3 oz

- Canned chicken: 21 g per 3 oz

- Roast chicken: 18 g per 3 oz

- Canadian bacon (if and where available): 15 g per 3 oz

- Chorizo: 21 g per 3 oz

- Pepperoni: 18 g per 3 oz

- Roast turkey breast: 18 g per 3 oz

- Beef jerky: 13 g per 1 oz

Plant-Based Protein

Considering the fact that not everyone eats meat, there are very good options for a more vegetarian diet. Some of the best examples are:

- Peanut butter: 8 g per 2 tbsp

- Quinoa: 8 g per cup

- Navy beans: 20 g per cup

- Lentils: 13 g per quarter cup

- Mixed nuts: 6 g per 2 oz

- Bean chips: 4 g per 1 oz

- Tofu: 12 g per 3 oz

- Edamame: 8 g per half cup

- Green peas: 8 g per cup

- Wheat germ: 6 g per 1 oz

- Soba noodles: 12 g per 3 oz

Although most of the terminology may seem confusing, they are not really and are quite straight forward. Most of this information can be found on packaging of the food items along with other nutritional information, including how to store them to preserve them for as long as possible. Some food items may contain ideas for recipes or how to use them if we do not already know.

- Measurement conversion:

1 oz equals 28.35 g and 0.063 lbs

Various liquids can be converted to and from milliliters, however not all liquids weigh the same in grams as their indication in weight, and different items' weight varies in comparison. It is advisable to follow weight as indicated and vice versa to prevent incorrect conversion.

Myths About Bodybuilding

The number one belief we humans probably have is that in order for us to gain body mass, we need to eat a lot and juice up on protein shakes and just about every recommendation from the experts. The truth is that we need all vitamins and nutrients to first build a balance of good health before we can start building body mass, losing weight, or strengthening our bodies.

This does not mean we should not utilize available resources to help us reach our goals, but we should not depend on these to get us to where we need to be. We still need to practice moderation by means of portion control and our daily intake amount of said portions. Creating a healthy diet with researched information and cross referencing details given to us by others practicing the same will always remain the best way to go.

Drinking water is also very important, and while learning that drinking eight glasses of water is a must, this is only true if our bodies require it, and for some people this is a good daily goal depending on daily activity. It is important to cleanse our bodies on a daily basis, but we should never drink more water than is needed because we could be flushing out many good bacterias in the process, which is not something we are trying to achieve. As a reference, we can refer to adults needing about 15 and a half cups of water a day. However, this is only meant as a reference for the average person and does not need to be followed to the tee.

Essential Equipment for Meal Prep

Knowing how to store food correctly can eliminate a lot of waste and also help to preserve important and essential nutritional value of food items, along with extending an item's shelf life for as long as it is still in good condition. Storing food correctly is another way to moderate portion intake and meal planning for the week (assuming you follow a weekly meal prep plan, but this will vary on personal choice and circumstance as well).

A significant loss of food is caused by incorrect food storage conditions and also decisions made at the much earlier stages of the food supply chain, which unfortunately predisposes food items to a much shorter shelf life. Efficient cold storage, for one, is extremely imperative to prevent food quality and quantity losses.

Before diving into storing food correctly, we should take a look at the three types of foods and how they interact with their different storage units or methods respectively.

• Perishable foods: Fresh vegetables, fruit, eggs, dairy, meat, and fish are all perishable, meaning that these food items need proper storage and care, otherwise they will go bad in as soon as a day for some food items, such as strawberries. These foods usually need to be stored in refrigerated or frozen temperatures in order to stay fresher and last longer. All food that is cooked is also classified as perishable, but can last much longer if kept at fridge or freezer temperatures.

- Semi-perishable foods: Food items such as dried fruits, dry mix, grains, and flour are semi-perishable items because they last very well and long if stored correctly; however, the possibility of the loss of quality of these foods over extended periods of time is also a reality.

- Non-perishable foods: Canned foods, spices, and dried beans are foods that have a long shelf life, but even these items can lose quality and spoil if not stored correctly. With all food storage methods, there are factors that may influence the longevity of foods, which is always something to keep in mind.

With the above said, we can now discuss pros of correct storage methods as well as the cons. This will definitely make meal planning a joy instead of a chore because we are getting to know our food so much better as well.

Materials for Storing Food

Freezing food, whether it is raw or cooked, is certainly the best way to save on wastage and is also good for planning ahead. Not only this, freezing food for future use saves money, time, and effort. Freezing food is also very easy and takes less effort than fermenting or canning foods. What is important to know, though, is how to store food items to freeze them without letting them spoil, as air can affect the longevity and quality of food items. Keep in mind that dry goods do not need to be frozen and this option is mostly aimed at fresh produce, raw meats, cooked food, and canned food items that have been opened. There are different storage materials for different foods and their benefits.

Freezer bags are very easy to use and come in different sizes and functions. Ziplock bags help to seal food with its zipping function, meaning that locking the freshness and essential nutrients of the food in the bag is an absolute breeze. The zipping function helps us to make sure that we can push out all the air that can contaminate foods, and without any air taking up space, aside from other reasons, means our items can be stored neatly without taking up too much space in the freezer.

One fantastic function of zipping bags is that we can store sauces and gravies as well without having to use large or expensive containers that will most likely take up a lot of storage space in the freezer. They can also be washed and reused again and again. The downside of these bags are that over time and multiple uses they can become less usable due to wear and tear over time, however this is still less expensive than buying containers. These bags are sold in packs of a variety of amounts, from 10 up to 100, and last very long. They also come in different sizes, so we can use smaller bags for smaller items such as portioned off fruits and cooked foods and larger ones for larger items, such as meats or fish.

Not all freezing bags feature a zipping function but are just as useful by tying a knot to close them, and most bags without the zipping function usually come with tools to close them without having to tie knots.

A very useful trick to get all the air out of the bag we want to freeze is to submerge the bag with the content we want to freeze in water with the opening of the bag above the waterline. This allows the air to escape easily before sealing it and has almost the same effect as vacuum-sealed bags, keeping items fresher for even longer.

Foods Not to Freeze

As much as freezing our food is beneficial, not all food can or should be frozen for various reasons. Soft greens such as lettuce contain a lot of water and will lose their texture and shape once thawed. However, they can be frozen if we are using them in smoothies. With this said though, using fresh soft greens for this purpose is always best. Fruits and vegetables we want to use for fresh salads such as tomatoes and cucumbers should also not be frozen. Tomatoes especially lose so much of their firmness and are not recommended for the freezer. These items should be kept in the fridge to make them last as long as possible. Avocados, potatoes, coffee, and some dairy products should not be frozen. It is always wise to refer to instructions on packaging for storing methods and temperatures if there are any.

Eggs are another food item that should not be frozen whole because the egg itself expands during the freezing process, which causes the shell to crack.

How to Properly Freeze and Thaw Foods Made From:
Meat, Fish, Fruits, Vegetables, Grains, and Sauces

Many of us prefer to store cooked food for later usage when we work out our meal planning, and also to save leftovers to be reused at a later time. While the act of putting food in the freezer is simple enough, there are important points we need to remember before proceeding.

Before we can freeze any cooked foods we need to make sure that the food items are cooled down properly before popping them in our amazing little ziplock bags and in the freezer. Foods that are frozen while not cool enough can spoil the food even in the freezer because the outer layer of the items will freeze quite quickly and not give enough time for the inside to cool and freeze along with the outer layer. Warm foods that are cooled at freezer temperatures also cause moisture to build up into condensation, and this spoils the food fairly quickly. Always remember to label and date any items being stored for later use, and it is advisable to store these foods in the coldest part of the freezer.

Solid foods such as baked products, meat, chicken, and fish are recommended to be wrapped in foil before putting them in their respective bags. Freezer temperatures should be −18 °C (0 °F) to maintain food quality. An important point to note is that freezing foods does not destroy any bacteria, molds, or yeast the foods contain, but it does slow down in their activity by miles and therefore foods should be stored undisturbed; freezer doors that do not seal as they should, for example, can compromise the quality and safety of the food.

Freezers also need enough air circulation, and overpacking the freezer is not a good idea because when our freezers are too packed, the cold air that is meant to keep our food safe cannot circulate as required and can spoil our food items as the freezing process slows down too much and in turn does not retain the quality and life of these items.

Foods can be frozen for an indefinite amount of time, but keep in mind that the longer our food remains frozen, the more flavor deteriorates. As we know that even food from the freezer can spoil, by packaging being damaged for example, it is imperative to discard such items and not put them to use at all because the bacteria buildup in the food can be very dangerous.

Food items should not be thawed at room temperatures, save for baked goods such as breads and muffins. Foods should be thawed slowly to ensure their safety.

The most popular method of thawing food is probably to use the defrost function on a microwave, and this is handy if we are in a hurry and quickly need to put something together. However, there are other methods that work very well in any other case.

Putting frozen foods in the fridge to thaw takes longer and can even be done overnight, but it is effective in keeping them fresher until it is time to use them. The only downside with this method is that bacteria can begin to build up while defrosting if the item is left in the water produced from thawing, so it is important to make sure the food does not live in this condition for too long by removing food out of the water.

If for some reason there is no space in the fridge or we need to thaw food quicker but are not in a hurry to use the microwave, putting these items in water outside the fridge works just as well and the same steps need to be followed as foods being thawed in the fridge for the same reasons. One more step in this method of defrosting is to put the food in the fridge after thawing to keep it cool for later use if not being used immediately. Thawed foods can last another day or two in the fridge, and longer if the foods are vacuum sealed.

It is up to each individual to determine which method works best for them to ensure food safety and aid in maintaining healthy eating habits over periods of time. When we plan ahead and prepare meals for future use, we can determine if we are going to do this on a weekly or monthly basis. Because food lasts longer if wrapped and stored correctly, the expiration date on frozen goods is far away and can lessen the amount of time spent preparing foods for this purpose in the long run.

Reheating food is very simple and does not really require any special treatment as most cooked foods can be heated up in the oven or in a pot over the stove until ready to eat.

Maximizing Efficiency:
Tips for Storing Food in Refrigerators and Freezers

Proper usage of your refrigerator and freezer ensures effective food preservation and energy efficiency. These two appliances have become integral to modern households. Yet, many overlook essential storage protocols, inadvertently wasting energy and compromising food quality.
The location of your refrigerator and freezer is paramount. An ideal spot is away from direct sunlight and significant heat sources like ovens or heaters. Moreover, it's essential to leave a gap of about 10 cm from the wall to facilitate optimal functioning of the cooling mechanism typically located at the back.

A temperature of 2-3 degrees Celsius is ideal for the refrigerator. Make a habit of inspecting the seals regularly to ensure they are intact, guaranteeing optimal sealing of your appliance. Minimizing the opening of the appliance's door conserves energy; this is especially true during power cuts where reduced access ensures longer freshness of the stored items.

When the walls start showing about 5-7 mm ice buildup, it's defrosting time.

Food placement also impacts the effectiveness of storage. Avoid transferring hot items directly into the refrigerator to prevent malfunction. Using specialized plastic bags or containers (plastic or glass) for storing food is advisable. Overcrowding the fridge might lead to inconsistent cooling, so always ensure ample space between items.

On the hygiene front:

1. Raw and cooked foods shouldn't mingle.
2. Be mindful of potential drips from foods like raw meats.
3. Preferably cook frozen items without prior thawing. If thawing is needed, do it inside the refrigerator. Using methods like countertop thawing can spur bacterial growth.
4. Use food wraps for dry and non-alcoholic items. Fatty foods are better with aluminum foil, but avoid using foil for acidic items.

Organizing food appropriately is crucial. Reserve the top shelves for eggs (lasting up to 4 weeks), followed by raw meat or fish (consumable within a few days) and fresh cheeses (5-10 days). Middle shelves can house deli meats (up to a week) and mature cheeses (typically in wax paper for around 2 weeks). Vegetables and fruits belong in the bottom drawers and are best when consumed within a week.

For freezers:

1. Only freeze fresh items.
2. Wait for cooked food to cool to room temperature before freezing.
3. Fish and fruits meant for freezing should be cleaned and dried first.
4. Pre-segment items like meat or fish before freezing to facilitate easy portioning later, as they should be consumed in one go after thawing.
5. Remember never to refreeze once thawed.

While packing for the freezer, ensure that bags are air-free and labeled, with contents and date. Take care with salt, as freezing can intensify its flavor. Avoid overfilling containers as the content expands upon freezing. Arrange containers strategically: along walls for horizontal freezers and at the top for chest freezers.

Optimal Food Preservation and Longevity

Ensuring food remains nutritious, flavorful, and safe hinges on proper storage techniques. By doing so, you not only enhance its shelf life but also curb wastage and guarantee healthful consumption. This section provides a deep dive into effective storage methods for various food categories, from produce to dairy, meats, and common pantry items.

Fruits:

- *Ambient Storage (like Citrus, Bananas, Tomatoes):* Best kept on kitchen counters but shielded from direct sunlight to attain peak ripeness.
- *Cool Storage (such as Berries, Grapes, Apples):* Place them in the refrigerator's freshness compartment for prolonged freshness.
- *For Seasonal Fruits:* Items like peaches and plums should rest at ambient temperature till they mature, post which they can be cooled.

Vegetables:

- *Shadowed, Cool Storage (for Potatoes, Onions, Garlic):* Ideal locations include cupboards or dark storage spaces.
- *Refrigerated Storage (including Leafy Veggies, Broccoli, Carrots):* The high-moisture compartment in fridges is best.

Dairy and Egg Guidance

Milk products and Yogurt: Best positioned on the central or top racks in the refrigerator where temperature consistency is maintained.
Eggs: Retain in the provided carton and place on the main shelves, steering clear of the door, which experiences temperature variances.

Meats and Aquatic Foods

Fresh Cuts and Birds: Occupy the refrigerator's lowest shelf, retaining the factory packaging to ward off cross-contamination.
Fish and Seafood: Locate them in the refrigerator's chilliest zone or atop an ice bed, ensuring consumption within a couple of days.
Frozen Varieties: Securely enclose and freeze. Minced meats remain good for 3-4 months, while entire portions stretch up to 12 months.

Essentials for the Pantry

Preserved Provisions: These thrive in cool, shaded regions, distant from heat exposure.
Staples such as Flour, Cereal, and Pasta: Airtight containment in a moisture-free, cool cupboard works best. Whole grain flours, however, benefit from refrigeration for longevity.
Oils: Ensure these are positioned away from light exposure to keep them fresh.

Emphasis on Food Safety

Dating: Mark perishables with storage dates to monitor freshness. Optimal Cooling: Retain refrigerator temperatures at 35-38°F (1.7-3.3°C) and freezers at 0°F (-18°C).
Aeration: Ensure the fridge and freezer aren't stuffed, promoting efficient temperature distribution.
Shelf Life Awareness: Prioritize usage before the 'best by' dates and stay vigilant for decay signs.

Adept food storage is a blend of both art and scientific insights, accentuating the essence and safety of the sustenance we partake daily. It necessitates a grasp of specific temperature needs, tailored storage for diverse food groups, and an alertness towards expiration timelines. Adopting these strategies, households can relish in more palatable, nutritious feasts, championing a sustainable and waste-minimizing approach. Be it the meticulous arrangement of dairy in fridges or the conscious handling of periodic produce, these pointers carve out the path to a streamlined kitchen and a wholesome lifestyle.

All-in-One Handbook to Safeguarding Foods: From Produce to Proteins and Beyond

Storing food isn't just about making room in your fridge or pantry; it's a blend of art and knowledge that respects each food item's particular demands. Recognizing the nuances of correct food preservation is key to maintaining its vitality, taste, and health benefits, and to reducing wastage. In this handbook, we unfold distinct storage techniques for different food kinds, like veggies, fruits, meats, dairy, bakery items, and herbs. These strategies are straightforward and suitable for households, engaging for both grown-ups.

Veggies Guide:

- *Carrots:* After peeling and slicing, submerge in water inside a sealed glass jar for extended freshness.
- *Greens:* Dry well post-wash, cushion with a moist paper towel, and put inside a zipper-lock bag or sealed container in the vegetable drawer.
- *Tomatoes:* Preserve ripe ones at ambient temperature, shielded from sun. Cold storage can diminish their taste.
- *Potatoes:* Keep in a breezy, dim location, not alongside onions.
- *Onions:* A dry, shaded area, away from potatoes.

- *Broccoli & Cauliflower:* In the veggie drawer, put inside a loose plastic bag.
- *Salad Greens:* Moist paper towel wrap, then in a zipper-lock bag.
- Cucumbers: Room temp or veggie drawer as preferred.
- *Peppers & Eggplant:* Cold storage.
- *Zucchini:* Keep chilled.
- *Mushrooms:* Use a paper sack in the fridge.
- *Garlic:* Store in a dim, cool spot.
- *Corn:* Keep chilled with its husk.
- *Asparagus:* Stand in water inside a glass.
- *Celery:* Aluminum foil wrap and chill.

Fruits Know-How:

- *Berries:* After a vinegar wash and drying, place on a paper-towel layer inside a ventilated container.
- *Apples:* In the fridge's vegetable drawer, isolated from other items to prevent premature ripening.
- *Bananas:* Prolong freshness by isolating and wrapping stems in cling wrap.
- *Oranges, Grapes, & Cherries:* Cold storage.
- *Peaches, Plums, Pears, Pineapple, Mango, Kiwi:* Let them mature outside, then refrigerate.
- *Melons & Watermelon:* Chilled for sliced pieces, else at room temperature.
- *Avocado:* Allow ripening, then refrigerate.
- *Citrus:* Store chilled inside a bag.

Meat & Seafood Suggestions:

- *Chicken & Red Meat:* Use the original packing or securely wrap. Store in the fridge's chilliest part or freeze for longer periods.
- *Fish:* Refrigerate on ice or freeze if not using immediately.
- *Beef, Pork, & Lamb:* Chilled or frozen storage in suitable wrap.
- *Shellfish:* A well-aerated container in the fridge.

Dairy Directives:

- *Cheese:* First in wax or parchment paper, then in a plastic wrap or bag.
- *Milk:* In its container, stored on the main refrigerator shelves.
- *Eggs & Butter:* Cold storage.
- *Yogurt:* Always refrigerate.

Bakery Bits:

- *Breads:* Slice and freeze if not consuming soon; toast directly when needed.

- *Pastries:* At room temp inside a sealed container or freeze portions for later.

Herbs Hints:

- *General:* Treat as fresh flowers; jar with water in the fridge or moist towel wrap in a sealed bag.
- *Basil:* In water at room temp.
- *Leafy Herbs:* Cold storage in water.
- *Hardy Herbs:* Damp towel wrap and stored cold.

Each edible has distinct care requirements. Correct processing and preservation methods can heighten their lifespan and quality. Home remedies can be engaging and potent, offering a fun approach to enlightening everyone about quality food, eco-friendly habits, and thoughtful eating. By tailoring your techniques to each food's requirements, you guarantee more delightful, fresher meals while conserving resources.

Temperature Zones in Your Fridge and Freezer

The different areas within your fridge and freezer have distinct temperature levels that determine how items should be stored:

- *Top Shelves:* These maintain a steady temperature, ideal for consistently cooled items such as dairy products.
- *Center Shelves:* Suitable for ready-to-eat meats, dairy products like cheese, and eggs.
- *Bottom Shelves:* Typically the chilliest sections, perfect for storing raw seafood and meat to inhibit bacterial development.
- *Freshness Drawers:* Tailored to manage humidity levels, these are best for produce that requires a certain moisture level.
- *Door Storage:* The temperature here can vary more frequently. Thus, it's best for items like sauces and items not highly affected by temperature shifts.

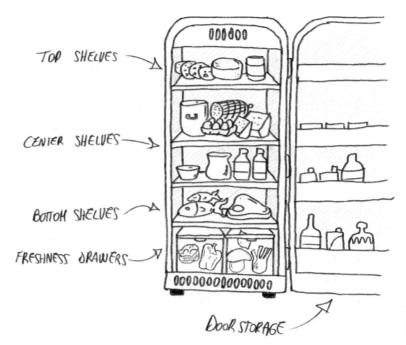

Safety with Raw Meats: To avoid the risk of raw meat juices contaminating other foods, place them on the lowest shelves.

Consistent Cooling for Eggs: The stable temperature in the fridge's central area helps retain the freshness of eggs, compared to the inconsistent temps at the door.

Humidity Control: Some refrigerators offer drawers with humidity control. High moisture levels benefit vegetables prone to wilting, whereas fruits and vegetables that decay rapidly benefit from a drier environment.

Freezer Tips: Arrange items based on when they'll be used. Frequent-use items at the front and others towards the back. Properly sealed items will stay free from freezer burn.

Ripening Gas: Certain fruits, including bananas and apples, emit ethylene, a gas that speeds up ripening. Store these separately to avoid affecting other items.

Avoiding Flavor Mix: Items like milk can pick up strong odors, so they should be kept away from pungent foods.

Eyes on Food: Position foods where they are visible to ensure they are used before going bad.

Realizing the distinct temperature and storage areas in your fridge and freezer ensures foods remain at their best in terms of taste, quality, and safety.

Menu Decisions: Craft menus around dishes that maintain their quality over days, such as roasts, casseroles, and cooked grains.

Ingredient Quality: Opt for fresh and high-quality ingredients for extended shelf life.

Pre-portioning: Pre-portion meals for convenience and to minimize the risk of spoilage.

Safety in Cooking: Always cook foods to the suggested internal temperatures to eradicate harmful bacteria.

Cool Before Storing: Cool hot dishes to room temperature before refrigerating to avoid condensation, which can cause spoilage.

Cook in Batches: Preparing large amounts and freezing in portions is especially effective for dishes like soups and stews.

Seal the Freshness: Use sealed containers to keep meals fresh. For longer storage durations, consider vacuum-sealing.

Date Your Food: Label each container with the preparation date to ensure it's consumed while fresh.

Texture Maintenance: If meals have varied textures, store components separately or layer them to retain their integrity.

Maximizing Freezer Use

Portion Freezing: Consider freezing meals for later consumption.

Safe Defrosting: Always thaw meals in the refrigerator to maintain quality and safety.

Safety First Expiration Awareness: Always be aware of how long meals have been stored and adhere to recommended storage durations.

Visual Inspection: Regularly check stored items for any signs of deterioration.

Preventing Contamination: Ensure raw and cooked foods are stored separately.

Achieving a week's worth of fresh meals using efficient planning and storage is both feasible and beneficial. Not only does it save on costs, but it also minimizes wastage. Adopting these methods regularly transforms our dietary habits into an intentional, delightful aspect of our routine. Instilling these values in youngsters can nurture a lasting respect for food and the environment.

Motivational

Staying positive and motivated during our transformations can become monotonous and boring, but remember that when we feel this way it is because we might slowly be mastering our current new habits. It might also feel like we are no longer making any progress, but that could simply mean that we have conquered a part of the goal we set out for ourselves and that we are still in the process of learning new things that continue to challenge us.

If we think about it in a way that we need to upgrade our skills to move forward and take a look at where we started and how far we have come, we can take a moment and give ourselves some well-deserved credit for our hard work.

In the end it doesn't matter what our goals are, because they will vary from one individual to the next. We do not have to become successful overnight to feel that we have accomplished anything. Something to avoid at all costs, however, is to compare our progress to any one other person, because this could demotivate us to continue if it seems like someone else is reaping more or faster rewards while they are putting in the same amount of effort.

We may not want to admit to this, but we do judge ourselves so harshly sometimes and this only ignites negativity and can make us want to give up, even when we are seeing results or have reached our smaller goals over a period of time.

The best we can do is do our best to stay positive and always keep our eyes on the prize. Remember, if we have come this far already, then we have already decided that taking on this journey is worth the effort and that the rewards in the end will probably be better than we might ever expect.

When it comes to taking out time to prepare meals, portion them, and save them for later, it can seem daunting as it might require much time to complete, but in the long run it saves time too because there is always food ready to be thawed and eaten when required.

With the correct information in conjunction with our dietary requirements and realistically set goals we can easily be successful in our health endeavors, whether we choose them to lose weight, gain muscle, or just get into and stay in our desired shape. Remember that maintaining a positive attitude can work miracles, even when we don't feel it every day.

High Protein Breakfast

1. Delicious Omelette

Preparation Time:	Cooking Time:	Serving
5 Minutes	2 Minutes	1

Ingredients

- 1 large egg
- 2 pinches of cinnamon
- 1 tbsp skimmed milk
- 3.5 oz. cottage cheese
- ½ tsp rapeseed oil
- 3/4 cup chopped strawberry, blueberries and raspberries

Directions

- Combine the egg, milk, and cinnamon in a mixing bowl. In a 7.87 inches (20cm) non-stick frying pan, heat the oil and pour in the egg mixture, turning it around to evenly coat the bottom. Cook for a few minutes, or until golden on the bottom. It's not necessary to turn it over.
- Place on a plate spread over cheese, then scatter with berries. Roll up and serve.

Nutrition Info

Calories: 264kcal

Carbohydrates: 18g

Protein: 22g

Fat: 12g

Sugars: 10g

Fibers: 4g

2. Banana Protein Pancakes

Preparation Time:	Cooking Time:	Serving
Minutes	15 Minutes	2

Ingredients

- 1 banana
- 3 large eggs
- 2/3 cup oats
- 1 tbsp baking powder
- 3 tbsp milk (dairy, soya, oat, or nut milk all work)
- ½ tsp. of cinnamon
- 2 tbsp protein powder (whey, pea, or whatever your preference)
- coconut oil, or a flavorless oil, for frying
- Peanut butter, maple syrup and berries or sliced banana to serve

Directions

- Whizz the banana, oats, eggs, milk, baking powder, cinnamon and protein powder in a blender for 1-2 mins until smooth. Check the oats have broken down, if not, blend for another minute.
- In a pan, heat a drizzle of oil. Pour or ladle in 2-3 rounds of batter, leaving space between each for spreading. Cook for 1-2 minutes, or until bubbles develop on top and the underside is golden. Cook for another minute on the other side, or until cooked through.
- Transfer to a warmed oven and repeat with the remaining batter. Serve in stacks with nut butter, maple syrup and fruit.

Nutrition Info

Calories: 422kcal

Carbohydrates: 30g

Protein: 31g

Fat: 15g

Sugars: Varies depending on amount used

Fiber: Varies depending on amount used

3. Feta Hash Scrambled Eggs

Preparation Time:	Cooking Time:	Serving
7 Minutes	8 Minutes	1

Ingredients

- 1 tsp snipped chives
- 2 tbsp coconut oil
- 3.5 oz. spinach
- 2 eggs, beaten
- 3/4 cup cherry tomatoes, halved
- 4 spring onions, chopped
- 2/3 cup feta, cut into small cubes

Directions

- In a nonstick pan, heat the oil over low-medium heat. Cook for 3-4 minutes, until the tomatoes and spring onions, are softened.
- Then add the feta and cook for 1 min to warm through, then pour in the eggs and chives. Season with pepper and keep stirring to scramble the eggs. Put a handful of the spinach on a plate and top it with the eggs.
- Serve the rest of the spinach on the side.

Nutrition Info

Calories: 462kcal

Carbohydrates: 5g

Protein: 32g

Fat: 22g

Sugars: 9g

Fiber: 5g

4. Healthy Black Bean with Avocado & Egg

Preparation Time:	**Cooking Time:**	**Serving**
5 Minutes	5 Minutes	2

Ingredients

- 2 large eggs
- 2 tsp. rapeseed oil
- ¼ tsp cumin seeds
- 1 red chili, deseeded and thinly sliced
- 1 large garlic clove, sliced
- 12 oz. can of black beans
- ½ 12 oz. can cherry tomatoes
- 1 lime, cut into wedges
- 1 small avocado, halved and sliced
- a handful of fresh, chopped coriander

Directions

- Firstly, Heat the oil in a large non-stick frying pan. Add the chili and garlic and cook until softened and starting to color. Break in the eggs on either side of the pan. Once they start to set, spoon the beans (with their juice) and the tomatoes around the pan and sprinkle over the cumin seeds. You're aiming to warm the beans and tomatoes rather than cook them.
- Turn off the heat and add the avocado and coriander to the pan. Half of the lime wedges should be squeezed over the top. The remaining wedges should be served on the side for squeezing over.

Nutrition Info

Calories: 355kcal

Carbohydrates: 17g

Protein: 20g

Fat: 14g

Sugars: 9g

Fiber: 20.9g

5. Spinach Green Eggs

Preparation Time:	Cooking Time:	Serving
5 Minutes	15 Minutes	2

Ingredients

- 2 large eggs
- 1 tbsp Greek yogurt
- 2 garlic cloves, sliced
- 2 tbsp rapeseed oil, plus a splash of extra
- 1 cup spinach
- 2 trimmed leeks, sliced
- ½ tsp coriander seeds & fennel seeds
- pinch of chili flakes, plus an extra to serve
- squeeze of lemon

Directions

- In a large frying pan, heat the oil. Cook until the leeks are tender, adding a pinch of salt. Combine the garlic, coriander, fennel, and chili flakes in a mixing bowl. Once the seeds have started to crackle, add the spinach and reduce the heat. Stir until the spinach has wilted and decreased, then scrape it to one side of the pan. Pour a small amount of oil into the pan, then crack in the eggs and fry until cooked to your liking.
- Stir the yogurt through the spinach mix and season. Pile onto two plates, top with the fried egg, squeeze over a little lemon and season with black pepper and chili flakes to serve.

Nutrition Info

Calories: 298kcal

Carbohydrates: 9g

Protein: 18g

Fat: 17g

Sugars: 9.1g

Fiber: 3.1g

6. Chicken Protein Waffles

Preparation Time:	Cooking Time:	Serving
5 Minutes	20 Minutes	6

Ingredients

- 1 Trifecta chicken breast (4oz)
- ½ tsp nutmeg
- 2 tbsp sugar-free syrup
- 1 cup protein waffle mix
- 3/4 cup unsweetened almond milk
- 3 tbsp egg whites
- ½ tsp cinnamon

Directions

- Pre-heat waffle iron and cover in non-stick cooking spray. In a bowl, whisk together waffle mix, seasoning, egg, and milk, until blended.
- Then dip chicken breast in the batter to form a thick coating and add to the air fryer. Cook for 10 to 12 minutes at 360 degrees Fahrenheit. Put the remaining batter on the waffle iron and cook according to instructions.
- Serve warm with your favorite toppings.

Nutrition Info

Calories: 403kcal

Carbohydrates: 35g

Protein: 43g

Fat: 7g

Sugars: Varies depending on the protein waffle mix used, please refer to the nutrition label on the product.

Fiber: 0.9g

7. Pesto Egg Sandwich

Preparation Time:	**Cooking Time:**	**Serving**
5 Minutes	15 Minutes	4

Ingredients

- 2 trifecta peeled hard-boiled egg (8 pack)
- thinly prosciutto, sliced
- 4 thin slices of cornbread
- pesto sauce
- 1 radish, thinly sliced
- 2 cheese slices
- slice up some of your favorite fruit (optional)

Directions

- Firstly, cut the cornbread into thick slices. Cut into thin slices: prosciutto, radish, and egg.
- Spread pesto over the cornbread slice.
- Add some prosciutto, and radish, then peeled hard-boiled egg slices and cheese slices. Enjoy with your favorite fruit or collards on the side.

Nutrition Info

Calories: 498kcal

Carbohydrates: 34g

Protein: 41g

Fat: 29g

Sugars: 1.64 g (excluding the optional fruit)

Fibers: 1.6 g

8. Grilled Sandwich with Mustard Green

Preparation Time:	Cooking Time:	Serving
10 Minutes	20 Minutes	4

Ingredients

- 1 large egg per sandwich
- 2 slices cornbread
- ½ cup grated or sliced cheddar cheese
- 2 tbsp butter
- salt and pepper to taste

Directions

- Place all of your ingredients, utensils, and pan (plus lid), and plate out before you start.
- Crack the egg into a small bowl. Turn the stove on to medium-low. If it's too hot it will burn the butter or cook the toast before the egg is cooked.
- Butter one side of each slice of cornbread. Then cut a hole out of one slice of cornbread. Keep the hole and toast it too.
- Place each slice of cornbread buttered side down in the skillet. While the cornbread is browning, butter the top side of the cornbread. Allow it to toast until lightly brown. Remove the slice of cornbread with the hole in it momentarily.
- Turn the slice of cornbread that's still in the pan (as well as the hole) and quickly put cheese on it. Return the slice of cornbread with the hole to the pan, press it down so that the egg doesn't seep under it and slide the egg out of the bowl and into the hole. Keep holding the cornbread for a couple of seconds for the egg to set.
- Get the lid on the pan and allow it to cook until the cornbread is toasted and the egg is cooked to your likely. Season the sandwich with salt and pepper and enjoy it with mustard greens or chips.

Nutrition Info

Calories: 453kcal

Carbohydrates: 29g

Protein: 31g

Fat: 27g

Sugars: 1.60 g

Fibers: 1.2 g

9. Candied Bacon

Preparation Time:	Cooking Time:	Serving
5 Minutes	20 Minutes	6

Ingredients

- ¼ cup packed brown sugar
- ground black pepper to taste
- ¼ pound thick-cut bacon

Directions

- Preheat oven to 350 degrees f (175 degrees C). Place bacon slices on a cooling rack set over a baking sheet, and put black pepper and brown sugar on it.
- Bake in the preheated oven for 10 minutes, turn slices and bake another 5 minutes until bacon is browned and crisp, about 20 to 30 minutes. Serve and enjoy!

Nutrition Info

Calories: 217kcal

Carbohydrates: 10g

Protein: 37g

Fat: 17g

Total sugars: 48 g

Fibers: 0.1 g

10. Black Bean Burritos

Preparation Time:	Cooking Time:	Serving
5 Minutes	10 Minutes	4

Ingredients

- 1 tbsp canola oil
- 3 tbsp onion, chopped
- 3 tbsp green pepper, chopped
- 1 can (15 oz) black beans, rinsed and drained
- 2 flour tortillas (8 inches), warmed
- 1 cup shredded cheese
- 1 medium tomato, chopped
- 1 cup shredded lettuce
- Optional toppings: Salsa, sour cream, minced fresh cilantro and cubed avocado

Directions

- In a nonstick skillet, heat oil over medium heat; sauté onion and green pepper until tender. Stir in beans; heat through.
- Spoon about ½ cup of vegetable mixture off-center on each tortilla. Sprinkle with the cheese, tomato and lettuce. Fold sides and ends over filling and roll up. Serve with optional toppings as desired.

Nutrition Info

Calories: 398kcal

Carbohydrates: 15g

Protein: 19g

Fat: 12g

Sugars: 6.32 g (excluding optional toppings)

Fibers: 15.4 g (excluding optional toppings)

11. Healthy Chick-Wrap

Preparation Time:	**Cooking Time:**	**Serving**
5 Minutes	10 Minutes	3

Ingredients

- ½ cup lemon juice
- 1/3 cup fish sauce
- 3 (6-inch) flour tortillas
- 4 cups shredded romaine lettuce
- ¼ cup sugar
- 2 cloves garlic, minced
- ¼ tsp crushed red pepper
- 1 cup grated carrots, (2 medium)
- 3 cups shredded cooked chicken, (12 oz)
- 1 large ripe tomato, cut into thin wedges
- 2/3 cup chopped scallions, (1 bunch)
- ⅔ cup slivered fresh mint

Directions

- Whisk lemon juice, fish sauce, sugar, garlic and crushed red pepper in a small bowl until the sugar is dissolved.
- Then, preheat oven to 325F. Wrap tortillas in foil and heat in the oven for 10 to 15 minutes, until softened and heated through. Keep warm.
- Combine lettuce, chicken, tomato, carrots, scallions and mint all in a large bowl. Add 1/3 cup of the dressing; toss to coat.
- Set out the chicken mixture, tortillas and the remaining dressing for diners to assemble wraps at the table.

Nutrition Info

Calories: 406kcal

Carbohydrates: 15g

Protein: 31g

Fat: 5g

Sugars: 15 g

Fibers: 8.3 g

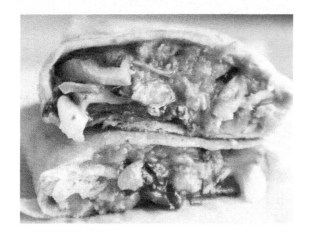

12. Lettuce Waldorf

Preparation Time:	Cooking Time:	Serving
15 Minutes	12 Minutes	4

Ingredients

- 2/3 cup whole meal penne
- 4 cooked chicken breasts (1.3 pounds or 600g), cut into bite-sized chunks
- 1 tbsp English mustard powder
- 2/3 cup black seedless grapes, halved
- 3 tsp sherry vinegar
- 2 x 4.2oz (120g) pots bio yogurt
- 4 spring onions, finely chopped
- 6 celery sticks (11.3oz or 320g), finely chopped
- 4 walnut halves, broken into pieces
- 8 crisp lettuce leaves from an iceberg lettuce

Directions

- Firstly, Boil the penne for 12 mins until done. Meanwhile, make a dressing by mixing the yogurt with the vinegar, mustard and spring onions. Add the celery, cooked penne and chicken to the dressing and stir until everything is well coated.
- Then add half the walnuts and grapes to half the salad and serve with half of the crisp lettuce leaves, either as a base or as lettuce wraps. Keep the remainder in the fridge, well covered, for up to three days, then add the nuts, grapes and lettuce or cabbage when ready to serve.

Nutrition Info

Calories: 452kcal

Carbohydrates: 27g

Protein: 45g

Fat: 11g

Sugars: 13.06 g

Fibers: 13 g

13. California Lettuce Wraps

Preparation Time:	**Cooking Time:**	**Serving**
10 Minutes	20 Minutes	4

Ingredients

- 1-pound lean ground beef
- ½ tsp salt
- ¼ tsp pepper
- 8 lettuce leaves
- 1/3 cup crumbled feta cheese
- 2 tbsp fat-free yogurt
- ½ medium ripe avocado, peeled and cut into 8 slices
- ¼ cup red onion, chopped
- cherry tomatoes, chopped (optional)

Directions

- In a large bowl, combine beef, salt and pepper, mixing lightly but thoroughly. Shape into eight 1/2-in.-thick patties.
- Grill patties, covered, over medium heat or broil 3-4 in. from heat until a thermometer reads 160°, 3-4 minutes on each side. Place patties in lettuce leaves. Combine feta and yogurt spread over patties. Top with avocado, red onion and tomatoes, if desired.

Nutrition Info

Calories: 253kcal

Carbohydrates: 5g

Protein: 25g

Fat: 13g

Sugar: 6.6g

Fiber: 9.9g

14. Air-Fryer Bacon Egg Cups

Preparation Time:	**Cooking Time:**	**Serving**
10 Minutes	15 Minutes	2

Ingredients

- 4 bacon strips
- 4 large eggs
- ¼ cup half-and-half cream
- 1/8 tsp pepper
- ½ cup cheddar cheese, shredded
- 2 green onions, chopped

Directions

- In a small skillet, cook bacon over medium heat until cooked but not crisp. Remove to paper towels to drain; keep warm.
- Preheat the air fryer to 350°. In a small bowl, whisk 2 eggs, cream and pepper. Wrap 2 bacon strips around the inside edges of each of two 8-oz. ramekins or custard cups coated with cooking spray.
- Sprinkle ramekins with half the cheese and onions. Divide egg mixture between ramekins. Break 1 remaining egg into each ramekin. Sprinkle with the remaining cheese and onions. Place ramekins on a tray in the air-fryer basket; cook until eggs are completely set, 15-20 minutes. Remove from the basket; let stand 5 minutes before serving.

Nutrition Info

Calories: 397kcal

Carbohydrates: 4g

Protein: 28g

Fat: 13g

Sugar: 3g

Fiber: 0.6g

15. Pesto Egg Sandwich

Preparation Time:	Cooking Time:	Serving
5 Minutes	15 Minutes	4

Ingredients

- 4 peeled hard-boiled egg
- 2 slices of whole-grain bread
- 2 tbsp pesto sauce
- 1 cucumber, thinly sliced
- 8 cheese slices
- thinly sliced prosciutto for garnish
- optional: slice up some of your favorite fruit (calories not included)

Directions

- Firstly, cut the bread into thick slices. Cut into thin slices: prosciutto, cucumber, and egg.
- Spread pesto over the bread slice. Add some prosciutto, and cucumber, then peeled hard-boiled egg slices and cheese slices.
- Enjoy with your favorite fruit or salad on the side.

Nutrition Info

Calories: 358kcal

Carbohydrates: 14g

Protein: 41g

Fat: 13g

Sugar: 5.5g

Fiber: 6.5g

16. Chorizo & Egg Burrito

Preparation Time:	Cooking Time:	Serving
5 Minutes	15 Minutes	4

Ingredients

- 4 eggs
- 10 ounces pork chorizo, casings removed
- 2 whole flour tortillas
- ½ avocado, halved, pitted, peeled, sliced
- 1 cup (or more) grated cheese

Directions

- Cook chorizo in a medium-sized pan, breaking it up as it cooks until it is thoroughly done (about 10 minutes). If required, drain any surplus fat.
- In a medium bowl whisk egg. Add eggs and half (5 ounces) of the cooked chorizo to a ziplock microwave cooking bag. Place in microwave for 2 ½ minutes. Warm tortillas in another Skillet until pliable (flexible).
- Divide cooked chorizo and egg mixture among tortillas. Top with avocado and cheese. Roll up tortillas. Wrap in parchment paper and store in ziplock storage bags.

Nutrition Info

Calories: 418kcal

Carbohydrates: 18g

Protein: 40g

Fat: 14g

Sugar: 2g

Fiber: 9g

17. Bacon Cheese Sandwich

Preparation Time:	Cooking Time:	Serving
10 Minutes	5 Minutes	1

Ingredients

- 1 slice of brown bread
- 1 cup cheddar cheese
- 3 cooked bacon strips
- 2 eggs
- 1 tbsp. coconut oil

Directions

- Put together bread, cheese and grilled bacon to make a sandwich. Grease the outside before pressing it into the waffle iron.
- Cook sandwich until golden brown. While this is cooking, prepare eggs to your liking. Top cooked sandwich with eggs and serve!

Nutrition Info

Calories: 389kcal

Carbohydrates: 14g

Protein: 42g

Fat: 13g

Sugar: 2g

Fiber: 2g

18. Beef Lettuce Rollups

Preparation Time:	Cooking Time:	Serving
5 Minutes	15 Minutes	2

Ingredients

- 10 oz. lean beef, cooked and shredded
- 4 leaf lettuce
- 2 dash black pepper

Directions

- Place a large slice of lettuce on a plate and top with beef.
- Sprinkle pepper over top and roll up. Repeat with remaining lettuce, beef, and pepper.
- Serve & enjoy!

Nutrition Info

Calories: 359kcal

Carbohydrates: 8g

Protein: 42g

Fat: 14g

Sugar: 0.5g

Fiber: 0.5g

19. Cauliflower Hash with Eggs

Preparation Time:	**Cooking Time:**	**Serving**
5 Minutes	15 Minutes	4

Ingredients

- 16 ounces turkey/ beef sausage
- 8 large eggs
- ⅛ tsp ground pepper
- 3 tbsp water
- ¼ tsp salt
- 6 ounces cauliflower rice
- 2 cloves garlic, minced
- 1 small onion, diced
- 4 tsp coconut oil, divided

Directions

- Heat oil in a large nonstick skillet over medium heat. Add onion and garlic; cook, stirring, until translucent. Add sausage; cook, stirring until cooked through, 4 to 5 minutes. Transfer the mixture to a plate.
- Increase the heat to medium-high and evenly distribute the cauliflower rice in the pan. Cook, without stirring, for 2 to 3 minutes, or until golden brown. Stir in the salt, pepper, and water after that. Cook, covered, for 3 to 4 minutes, or until tender and brown. Return the sausage mixture to the pan and heat for another 2 minutes.
- Heat tsp oil in a medium nonstick skillet over medium heat. Break 4 eggs into the pan and cook until the whites are set but the yolks are still runny, about 3 minutes (or up to 5 minutes for firmer yolks). Transfer to a plate and repeat with the remaining 1 tsp oil and the remaining 4 eggs.
- Divide the hash among 4 plates and top each with 2 fried eggs.

Nutrition Info

Calories: 367kcal

Carbohydrates: 15g

Protein: 43g

Fat: 14g

Fiber: 3.1g

Sugar: 5g

20. Protein-Rich Eggs

Preparation Time:	Cooking Time:	Serving
5 Minutes	15 Minutes	2

Ingredients

- 8 large eggs
- 2 oz cheese
- 1 tsp mustard
- ½ cup mayonnaise
- ⅛ tsp salt
- ⅛ tsp pepper

Directions

- Place eggs in a pot with enough water to cover them. Bring to a boil, then reduce to low heat and cook for 1-2 minutes. Cover and set aside for 10-14 minutes after removing from the heat.
- Peel eggs, slice them in half and add the yolk to a bowl. Use a fork to mash and mix the yolk with mayonnaise, mustard, salt, and pepper.
- Spoon in yolk mix to your egg white.
- Sprinkle with paprika, and cheese and top with fresh parsley for garnish. (Optional)

Nutrition Info

Calories: 313kcal

Carbohydrates: 1g

Protein: 38g

Fat: 9g

Sugar: 2g

High Protein First Courses

21. Healthy Cobb Salad

Preparation Time:	Cooking Time:	Serving
5 Minutes	15 Minutes	12

Ingredients

- 1 loaf, of sliced cornbread
- 1/2 cup balsamic vinaigrette
- 5 oz fresh baby spinach (about 6 cups)
- 1-1/2 pounds sliced deli ham
- 4 hard-boiled large eggs, finely chopped
- 8 bacon strips, cooked and crumbled
- ½ cup crumbled cheese
- 1 cup cherry tomatoes, chopped

Directions

- Cut loaf of cornbread in half lengthwise; hollow out top and bottom, leaving a 3/4-in. shell (save removed cornbread for another use). Brush vinaigrette over cornbread halves.
- Layer spinach, ham, eggs, bacon, cheese and tomatoes on the cornbread bottom. Replace top. Cut loaf in half lengthwise from top to bottom; cut crosswise 5 times to make 12 pieces. You can also add some collards with ham.

Nutrition Info

Calories: 239kcal

Carbohydrates: 17g

Protein: 18g

Fat: 9g

Sugar: 23g

Fiber: 7g

22. Citrus Salmon Papillote

Preparation Time:	Cooking Time:	Serving
15 Minutes	15 Minutes	6

Ingredients

- 6 (4 ounces each) salmon fillets
- 1-pound fresh asparagus, trimmed and halved
- olive oil-flavored cooking spray
- 6 orange slices
- 6 lime slices
- ½ tsp salt
- ¼ tsp pepper
- 2 tbsp minced fresh parsley
- 3 tbsp lemon juice

Directions

- Preheat oven to 425°. Cut parchment or heavy-duty foil into six 15x10-in. pieces; fold in half. Arrange citrus slices on 1 side of each piece. Top with fish and asparagus. Spritz with cooking spray. Sprinkle with salt, pepper and parsley. Drizzle with lemon juice.
- Fold parchment over fish; draw edges together and crimp with fingers to form tightly sealed packets. Place in baking pans.
- Bake until fish flakes easily with a fork, 12-15 minutes. Open packets carefully to allow steam to escape. Serve and enjoy your meal!

Nutrition Info

Calories: 224kcal

Carbohydrates: 6g

Protein: 24g

Fat: 10g

Fiber: 11g

Sugar: 21g

23. Chicken with Apple, Onion, and Cider Sauce

Preparation Time:	Cooking Time:	Serving
5 Minutes	20 Minutes	4

Ingredients

- 4 skinless, boneless chicken breasts (about 1/2 pound each)
- salt and pepper
- all-purpose flour for coating the chicken breasts
- 2 to 3 tbsp vegetable oil
- 1 large red onion, cut into large chunks
- 1 sweet cooking apple, cut into large chunks
- 3 tbsp apple cider vinegar
- 1 1/2 cups chicken broth
- 2 tsp. chicken base, such as better than bouillon, optional
- 2 tbsp cold unsalted butter
- 1 handful of chopped fresh parsley

Directions

- Heat the oven to 350 degrees F.
- Season the chicken breasts with salt and pepper and coat them with flour. Shake off any excess. Heat a 12-inch skillet over medium heat and add 2 tbsp of vegetable oil. When the oil is shimmering, add the chicken, and cook until golden brown, about 5 minutes a side. Transfer the chicken to a baking dish and place them in the oven for about 8 minutes, until cooked through.
- Meanwhile, add another tbsp of oil to the pan, and add the onions and apple. Increase the heat to medium-high and cook, stirring regularly, for about 2 minutes. Add the vinegar and scrape up any browned bits with a wooden spoon. Let the mixture boil for about a minute. Add the chicken broth and optional chicken base, and bring to a boil. Cook until the broth reduces by half. Remove the pan from the heat and stir in the butter. Season with salt and pepper.
- Remove the chicken from the oven and place each one on a dinner plate. Add the apples and onions, and spoon the sauce over each piece of chicken. Sprinkle with parsley.

Nutrition Info

Calories: 349kcal

Carbohydrates: 26g

Protein: 29g

Fat: 9g

Fiber: 10g

Sugar: 30g

24. Salmon with Pearl Couscous Salad

Preparation Time:	Cooking Time:	Serving
5 Minutes	15 Minutes	4

Ingredients

- 6-ounce pieces of skinless salmon fillet
- 1 cup pearl couscous
- 1 small shallot, thinly sliced
- 1 small bulb fennel, thinly sliced
- ½ tbsp. chopped fennel fronds
- 2 tbsp. olive oil
- 1 tbsp. fresh lemon juice
- ½ cucumber & chili halved lengthwise and thinly sliced
- salt and black pepper

Directions

- Prepare the couscous according to the package directions. In a large mixing bowl, combine the couscous, fennel, cucumber, shallot, lemon juice, 2 tbsp oil, salt, and pepper.
- Meanwhile, heat the remaining tbsp of oil in a large nonstick skillet over medium-high heat. Season the salmon with salt and pepper and sprinkle with the fennel fronds. Cook until opaque throughout, 3 to 5 minutes per side.
- Serve with the couscous salad.

Nutrition Info

Calories: 462kcal

Carbohydrates: 32g

Protein: 41g

Fat: 17g

Sugars: 8g

Fibers: 6g

25. Chili Salmon with Chopped Salad

Preparation Time:	Cooking Time:	Serving
10 Minutes	15 Minutes	4

Ingredients

- 1 lb. salmon piece
- 2 yellow peppers, diced
- 1 tbsp sea salt
- 2 tbsp red wine vinegar
- olive oil spray
- 1 tbsp olive oil
- 1 red onion, diced
- 1 cucumber, diced
- 4 celery stalks, diced
- 4 plum tomatoes, diced
- 16 olives, pitted and quartered

Directions

- Cut the salmon into quarters. Sprinkle the surface of the salmon with the chili salt then leave it in the fridge for an hour. Whisk the red wine vinegar and olive oil in a bowl, and season. Add the salad ingredients and toss.
- Preheat oven to 428°F or gas 7. Place the salmon skin-side down on a baking sheet lined with baking paper. Spray with oil and bake for 10 minutes, or until just done. Serve alongside the salad.

Nutrition Info

Calories: 409kcal

Carbohydrates: 9g

Protein: 28g

Fat: 12g

Sugars: 33g

Fiber: 12g

26. Best Deviled Eggs

Preparation Time:	**Cooking Time:**	**Serving**
2 Minutes	26 Minutes	12

Ingredients

- ½ cup mayonnaise
- 2 tbsp. milk
- 1 tsp dried parsley flakes
- ½ tsp minced chives
- ½ tsp ground mustard
- ¼ tsp salt
- ¼ tsp paprika
- 1/8 tsp garlic powder
- 1/8 tsp pepper
- 12 hard-boiled large eggs
- minced fresh parsley and additional paprika

Directions

- In a small bowl, combine all ingredients. Cut eggs lengthwise in half; remove yolks and set whites aside. In another bowl, mash yolks; add to the mayonnaise mixture, mixing well. Spoon or pipe filling into egg whites.
- Sprinkle with parsley and additional paprika. Serve with or without cornbread and mustard greens!

Nutrition Info

Calories: 75kcal

Carbohydrates: 2g

Protein: 4g

Fat: 6g

Sugars: 6g

Fiber: 0.7g

27. Chicken Lime Salad

Preparation Time:	Cooking Time:	Serving
5 Minutes	0 Minutes	1

Ingredients

- 1 can (4 oz.) canned chicken
- 1 oz. cheese
- 1.5 tbsp avocado oil
- 4 large lettuce leaf
- 2 tbsp. lime juice
- Salt as per taste

Directions

- Combine the chicken, cheese, lime juice, and salt (squeeze of lime juice and salt to taste).
- Arrange the lettuce leaves and top them with the chicken salad. Enjoy your snack!

Nutrition Info

Calories: 342kcal

Carbohydrates: 8g

Protein: 44g

Fat: 12g

Sugars: 2g

Fiber: 2g

28. Egg Parmesan Chaffles

Preparation Time:	**Cooking Time:**	**Serving**
5 Minutes	10 Minutes	2

Ingredients

- 8 large eggs
- 1 cup mozzarella cheese, shredded
- 1/3 cup grated parmesan cheese
- ½ tsp. Italian seasoning
- 1 tbsp coconut oil
- 1 clove garlic (minced, or use 1/2 clove for milder garlic flavor)
- ¼ tsp. baking powder (optional)

Directions

- Firstly, preheat your mini waffle iron for about 5 minutes, until hot. Stir in all other remaining ingredients (except toppings, if any).
- Pour enough chaffle batter into the waffle maker to completely cover the bottom. Cook until browned and crispy, about 3-4 minutes.
- Carefully remove the chaffle from the maker and set it aside to crisp up more. Serve crispy chaffles!

Nutrition Info

Calories: 342kcal

Carbohydrates: 5g

Protein: 41g

Fat: 15g

Sugars: 3g

Fiber: 0.1g

29. Chicken & Tomato Salad

Preparation Time:	Cooking Time:	Serving
5 Minutes	0 Minutes	1

Ingredients

- 2 tbsp coriander seeds, lightly crushed
- 5 oz. chicken breast, cooked and sliced
- 1 tbsp avocado oil
- 1 tbsp. mayonnaise
- ½ cup tomato

Directions

- In a bowl, combine all of the ingredients and thoroughly mix them.
- Serve & enjoy!

Nutrition Info

Calories: 318kcal

Carbohydrates: 7g

Protein: 46g

Fat: 14g

Sugars: 2.7g

Fiber: 3g

30. Miso & Sesame Eggs

Preparation Time:	Cooking Time:	Serving
5 Minutes	10 Minutes	2

Ingredients

- 1 tsp white miso
- 8 eggs
- 3 oz. cheese
- ½ tsp smoked paprika
- 2 tsp toasted sesame seeds

Directions

- Hard-boil the eggs for 10 mins then cool under running water. When cool enough to handle, carefully remove the shells.
- Cut the egg in halves and remove the yolks into a small bowl. To make a creamy consistency, add a dash of water to the miso, and cheese and mash them together. Return the mixture to the eggs, distribute the seeds on top, and finish with the paprika. Serve and enjoy!

Nutrition Info

Calories: 342kcal

Carbohydrates: 2g

Protein: 41g

Fat: 12g

Sugars: 1.5g

Fiber: 0.8g

31. Tomato Poult Salad

Preparation Time:	Cooking Time:	Serving
50 Minutes	Minutes	1

Ingredients

- 2 tbsp coriander seeds, lightly crushed
- 1 can chicken
- 1 tbsp. mayonnaise
- ½ can (12oz.) corn
- ½ tomato

Directions

- In a bowl, combine all of the ingredients and thoroughly mix them. Serve & enjoy!

Nutrition Info

Calories: 252kcal

Carbohydrates: 17g

Protein: 35g

Fat: 6g

Sugars: 9g

Fiber: 5.6g

32. Easy Chicken Lime Salad

Preparation Time:	**Cooking Time:**	**Serving**
50 Minutes	Minutes	1

Ingredients

- 1 can (5 oz.) canned chicken
- 4 large lettuce leaf
- 2 tbsp. lime juice
- Salt as per taste

Directions

- Combine the chicken, lime juice, and salt (squeeze of lime juice and salt to taste).
- Arrange the bib lettuce leaves and top them with the chicken salad. Enjoy your snack!

Nutrition Info

Calories: 242kcal

Carbohydrates: 8g

Protein: 32g

Fat: 10g

Sugars: 2g

Fiber: 2g

33. Spinach-Strawberry Salad with Walnuts

Preparation Time:	Cooking Time:	Serving
10 Minutes	5 Minutes	4

Ingredients

- 1 ½ tbsp extra-virgin olive oil
- 1 tbsp best-quality balsamic vinegar
- 2 tsp finely chopped shallot
- ¼ tsp salt
- ¼ tsp ground pepper
- 6 cups baby spinach
- 1 cup strawberries, sliced
- ¼ cup crumbled feta cheese
- ¼ cup toasted walnuts, chopped

Directions

- Whisk oil, vinegar, shallot, salt and pepper in a large bowl. Let stand for 5 to 10 minutes to allow shallots to soften and mellow a bit.
- Add spinach, strawberries, feta and walnuts to the bowl and toss to coat with the dressing.

Nutrition Info

Calories: 158kcal

Carbohydrates: 6g

Protein: 5g

Fat: 12g

Sugars: 13g

Fiber: 9g

34. Asian Salad

Preparation Time:	Cooking Time:	Serving
15 Minutes	2 Minutes	4

Ingredients

- 1 (8-ounce) can of sliced water chestnuts, drained
- 8 ounces snow peas, blanched
- 2 jarred roasted red peppers or pimientos
- 2 tsp reduced-sodium soy sauce
- 2 tsp toasted sesame oil

Directions

- Combine water chestnuts and snow peas in a medium bowl.
- Puree roasted red peppers (or pimientos) with soy sauce and oil. Pour over the vegetables and toss to combine.

Nutrition Info

Calories: 69kcal

Carbohydrates: 7g

Protein: 4g

Fat: 4g

Sugars: 3g

Fiber: 4g

35. Mediterranean White Bean Salad

Preparation Time:	Cooking Time:	Serving
10 Minutes	0 Minutes	4

Ingredients

- 1 (15 fluid ounces) can of cooked white beans drained & rinsed
- 2 mini cucumbers, chopped
- 1-2 tbsp red onion, chopped
- ½ red bell pepper, chopped
- 2 little tomatoes (grape, cherry, etc.) halved
- 1/3 cup olives pitted & chopped
- 1 tbsp fresh parsley chopped
- ½ tsp dried oregano
- 1 tbsp olive oil
- 1 tbsp vinegar/ lemon juice
- salt & pepper to taste

Directions

- Add all ingredients to a salad bowl and toss. Adjust ingredients as needed (e.g., more oil or vinegar). Serve & enjoy!

Nutrition Info

Calories: 234kcal

Carbohydrates: 21g

Protein: 12g

Fat: 9g

Sugars: 4g

Fibers: 9g

36. Cucumber Salad with Cashewnuts

Preparation Time:	Cooking Time:	Serving
15 Minutes	0 Minutes	4

Ingredients

- 2 cups cucumber, cut into strips
- ½ cup chopped coriander
- ½ cup roasted and crushed cashew nuts
- 1 tbsp chili-garlic paste
- 1 ½ tbsp lemon juice
- 1 ½ tsp soy sauce
- 1/2 tbsp red chilies flakes
- salt to taste

Directions

- Combine all the ingredients in a bowl and mix well. Serve & enjoy!

Nutrition Info

Calories: 103kcal

Carbohydrates: 8g

Protein: 6g

Fat: 5g

Fiber: 6g

Sugars: 7g

37. Cilantro Tofu Soup

Preparation Time:	Cooking Time:	Serving
5 Minutes	10 Minutes	2

Ingredients

- 1 tsp olive oil
- ½ cup fresh cilantro, chopped
- ¼ cup carrots, chopped
- ¼ cup broccoli florets
- 1 cup extra firm chopped tofu (drained)
- 2 cups vegetable broth
- 1 tbsp low sodium soy sauce
- ¼ tsp crushed black pepper
- ½ tsp lemon juice
- salt as per taste

Directions

- In a sauce pan heat oil and add cilantro. Sauté for 30 seconds. Add carrots and broccoli and sauté for another 30 seconds.
- Add tofu and sauté again for 30 seconds to one minute. Add vegetable broth, soy sauce, black pepper, lemon juice and salt.
- Cook uncovered on a medium flame for 5-7 minutes. Serve warm and garnish with more chopped cilantro.

Nutrition Info

Calories: 125kcal

Carbohydrates: 6g

Protein: 12g

Fat: 8g

Sugars: 3g

Fiber: 4g

38. Healthy Wonton Soup

Preparation Time:	**Cooking Time:**	**Serving**
15 Minutes	15 Minutes	8

Ingredients

- 8 cups no sodium chicken stock
- 1-pound lean ground pork
- 2 tbsp coconut aminos
- 1 tbsp sesame oil
- 1 tbsp ginger, finely chopped
- 2 cloves garlic, finely chopped
- 4 ounces spinach
- ½ cup sliced mushrooms
- ½ tsp salt
- 1/8 tsp pepper
- ½ cup bean sprouts optional and not counted in nutritional info
- ¼ cup green onions sliced (optional and not counted in nutritional info)

Directions

- Bring the bone broth or chicken stock to a boil in a large pot.
- In the meantime, blend the ground pork with the coconut aminos, sesame oil, ginger, garlic, and a pinch of salt.
- When the broth is boiling, drop 1 tbsp size meatballs of the pork mixture into the broth.
- Simmer for 3-4 minutes. Add the thinly sliced mushrooms and spinach. Allow simmering for another 2 minutes. Season with salt and pepper and garnish. Serve and enjoy!

Nutrition Info

Calories: 216kcal

Carbohydrates: 5g

Protein: 15g

Fat: 12g

Sugars: 1.2g

Fibers: 2.5g

39. Easy Chicken Pot Pie Soup

Preparation Time:	Cooking Time:	Serving
15 Minutes	15 Minutes	6

Ingredients

- 3 cups cauliflower florets
- 1 tsp dried onion flakes
- 1 cup frozen vegetables
- 8 oz cooked chopped chicken or turkey
- 2 tsp Better than Bouillon dissolved in 1 cup of hot water (or 1 cup of chicken broth too)
- 2 tbsp nutritional yeast (can sub with parmesan cheese)
- 1 tsp crushed garlic
- 2 tbsp olive oil
- ¼ tsp sage
- ¼ tsp thyme

Directions

- In a pot add cauliflower and enough water to almost cover the florets. Cover and cook until cauliflower is tender.
- Once the cauliflower is tender drain but retain the water. Add the cauliflower to a blender or food processor. To that add the olive oil, yeast, sage, thyme, garlic, dehydrated onions, a pinch of salt & pepper and ¼ cup of the cooking liquid. Puree until smooth.
- For The Soup: Add frozen vegetables to the pan and sauté a minute or two until warmed through. Add the chicken and stir. Then mix the bouillon with 1 cup of hot water and stir in. Add pureed cauliflower mixture to the cooked chicken and veggies.
- Cook until flavors meld, about 5 minutes. If it's too thick add more water or chicken broth until you get the consistency you like. Enjoy!

Nutrition Info

Calories: 143kcal

Carbohydrates: 8g

Protein: 15g

Fat: 2g

Sugars: 5g

Fiber: 6g

40. Lettuce, Orange and Spinach Salad

Preparation Time:	Cooking Time:	Serving
10 Minutes	0 Minutes	5

Ingredients

- 2 cups lettuce, torn into pieces
- 3/4 cup orange segments
- 1 cup spinach, roughly chopped
- 1 cup bean sprouts
- ½ cup spring onions (whites and greens), chopped

Dressing

- 1 tbsp lemon juice
- 1 tsp olive oil
- salt and freshly ground black pepper to taste

Directions

- Combine all the salad ingredients in a deep bowl and mix well.
- Add the dressing and toss well. Serve immediately.

Nutrition Info

Calories: 41kcal

Carbohydrates: 6g

Protein: 3g

Fat: 2g

Sugars: 15g

Fibers: 7g

High Protein Main Courses

41. Sesame Steak with Asparagus

Preparation Time:	**Cooking Time:**	**Serving**
10 Minutes	25 Minutes	6

Ingredients

- 3 tbsp reduced-sodium soy sauce
- 1 pound beef round steak
- 4 cups cut fresh asparagus
- 2 tbsp sesame oil
- 1 tbsp rice vinegar
- ½ tsp grated gingerroot
- 1 tsp sesame seeds

Optional: lettuce leaves, julienned carrot and radishes, cilantro leaves and lime wedges

Directions

- Preheat broiler. Place steak on a broiler pan. Broil 2-3 in. from heat until meat reaches desired doneness (for medium-rare, a thermometer should read 135°), 6-7 minutes per side. Let stand for 5 minutes before slicing.
- In a large saucepan, bring ½ in. water to a boil. Add asparagus; cook, uncovered, just until crisp-tender, 3-5 minutes. Drain and cool.
- Combine meat and asparagus with soy sauce, sesame oil, vinegar, and ginger. Sprinkle sesame seeds on top. If desired, serve over lettuce with carrot, radishes, cilantro and lime wedges.

Nutrition Info

Calories: 160kcal

Carbohydrates: 5g

Protein: 19g

Fat: 11g

Fibers: 4 grams

42. Delicious Garlic Chicken

Preparation Time:	Cooking Time:	Serving
10 Minutes	25 Minutes	6

Ingredients

- 1-1/2 pounds boneless skinless chicken thighs
- ½ tsp salt
- ¼ tsp pepper
- 1 tbsp olive oil
- 10 garlic cloves, peeled and halved
- 2 tbsp brandy or chicken stock
- 1 cup chicken stock
- 1 tsp fresh rosemary, minced
- ½ tsp fresh thyme, minced
- 1 tbsp fresh chives, minced

Directions

- Firstly, sprinkle salt and pepper on the chicken. In a large cast iron or other heavy skillets, heat oil over medium-high heat. Brown chicken on both sides. Remove from pan.
- Remove skillet from heat; add halved garlic cloves and brandy/ stock. Return to heat; cook and stir over medium heat until liquid is almost evaporated 1-2 minutes.
- Stir in stock, rosemary and thyme; return chicken to pan. Bring to a boil. Reduce heat; simmer, uncovered until a thermometer reads 170°, 6-8 minutes. Sprinkle with chives.

Nutrition Info

Calories: 203kcal

Carbohydrates: 2g

Protein: 21g

Fat: 12g

Fiber: 3g

43. Healthy Salmon with Veggies

Preparation Time:	**Cooking Time:**	**Serving**
10 Minutes	30 Minutes	4

Ingredients

- 1 (4 ounces) jar of pitted kalamata olives
- 4 fillets of salmon
- 1 tbsp soy sauce
- 1 large tomato, chopped
- 1 onion, chopped
- ½ cup capers
- 2 tbsp olive oil
- 1 tbsp lemon juice
- salt and pepper to taste

Directions

- Preheat the oven to 350 degrees F (175 degrees C). Place salmon fillets on a large sheet of aluminum foil and season with soya sauce. Combine tomato, onion, olives, capers, olive oil, lemon juice, salt, and pepper in a bowl.
- Spoon the tomato mixture over the salmon. To make a huge packet, carefully seal all of the foil's edges. Place the packet on a baking sheet. Bake for 30 to 40 minutes in a preheated oven until the fish flakes easily with a fork. Then remove from oven and serve.

Nutrition Info

Calories: 432kcal

Carbohydrates: 9.2g

Protein: 31g

Fat: 11g

Sugars: 2.5 grams

Fibers: 4 grams

44. Lemon Chicken Skewers

Preparation Time:	**Cooking Time:**	**Serving**
20 Minutes	25 Minutes	4

Ingredients

- 4 cornbread or pittas
- 2cm piece ginger, grated
- 1 lettuce, sliced
- 1 cup mint, leaves picked
- 1 lemon, zested and juiced
- ½ tsp ground cumin & ground coriander
- 4 skinless chicken breasts, each cut into 6 pieces
- 1 small red onion, sliced, to serve
- Pickled cabbage, kale, broccoli, chili sauce and hummus, to serve (all optional)
- 2/3 cup natural yogurt, plus extra to serve (optional)
- 4 metal or wooden skewers

Directions

- Finely chop half of the mint and combine it with the yogurt, half of the lemon juice, and all of the lemon zest, spices, and ginger in a mixing bowl. Mix well and season with a bit of salt and a lot of black pepper. Add the chicken pieces, stir well, and chill for 20-30 minutes. Meanwhile, soak 4 large wooden skewers for at least 20 minutes in water (or use metal ones).
- When you're ready to cook the chicken, heat your grill to medium heat and line the grill tray with foil. Thread the chicken onto the soaked wooden or metal skewers and grill for 15-20 mins, turning halfway through, until browned and cooked through.
- Warm the cornbread under the grill for a couple of seconds, then serve them topped with the lettuce, chicken, red onion, remaining lemon juice and mint, and any optional extras such as extra yogurt or pickled cabbage, chili sauce and hummus.

Nutrition Info

Calories: 362kcal

Carbohydrates: 38g

Protein: 41g

Fat: 4g

Sugars: 7g

Fiber: 6g

45. Turkey Lunch Bowl

Preparation Time:	Cooking Time:	Serving
15 Minutes	15 Minutes	2

Ingredients

- 5 oz. green lentils, drained
- 1 cup diced turkey breast
- 2 tsp balsamic vinegar
- 1 red pepper, quartered and sliced
- 1 red onion, halved and thinly sliced
- 1 lemon, zested and juiced
- 3 tbsp rapeseed oil
- 2 clementine, 1 zested and the flesh chopped
- 2 garlic cloves, chopped
- small handful of mint, chopped
- 3 walnut halves, broken

Directions

- Combine the onion and lemon juice in a mixing dish. Combine the turkey, half of the oil, the lemon and clementine zest, and the garlic in a mixing bowl.
- Tip the lentils into two bowls or lunchboxes and drizzle over the balsamic vinegar. Heat the remaining oil in a large non-stick wok, add the pepper, and stir-fry for 3 mins. Now add the turkey and half the onion and continue frying until the turkey is cooked and the pepper is tender. Pile on top of the lentils then add the clementine flesh, remaining onion, mint and walnut pieces.

Nutrition Info

Calories: 452kcal

Carbohydrates: 30g

Protein: 42g

Fat: 14g

Sugars: 49g

Fiber: 25g

46. Pesto Courgette Wedges

Preparation Time:	**Cooking Time:**	**Serving**
10 Minutes	20 Minutes	2

Ingredients

- 2 courgettes (about 11oz/300g, sliced into rounds)
- 5 large eggs
- 1 tbsp olive oil
- 10 cherry tomatoes
- 1 large garlic clove, finely grated
- 2 tbsp fresh pesto (choose one with whole pine nuts)
- handful of rockets

Directions

- Firstly, heat olive oil in a non-stick frying pan about 9.84 inc across, add the courgette slices and cook for 5 mins until softened, stirring occasionally. Meanwhile, beat the eggs with seasoning and the garlic in a large bowl.
- Remove the courgettes from the pan and wipe it clean with paper towels. Return the pan to heat and add the remaining oil. Stir the courgettes into the eggs, then pour into the frying pan and cook for 10 minutes over low heat, or until almost set. Slide onto a big dish, then return to the pan and cook the other side for a few seconds to set the remaining amount of raw egg. Remove from the pan and place on a cutting board.
- Tip the tomatoes into the pan for 2-3 mins to soften a little and char the skins. Cut the tortilla in half widthways, spread one half with 2 tbsp pesto, then top with the other half. Cut into wedges and top with the remaining pesto, the tomatoes and the rocket.

Nutrition Info

Calories: 449kcal

Carbohydrates: 9g

Protein: 26g

Fat: 17g

Sugars: 14g

Fiber: 8g

47. Butter Chicken

Preparation Time:	Cooking Time:	Serving
5 Minutes	4 Hours	6

Ingredients

- 3 medium chicken breasts
- 8 oz. carrots/tomatoes
- 21 oz. butternut squash
- 1 tbsp garam masala
- 1 small onion
- ½ tsp turmeric
- 1 tsp paprika
- 1 tsp garlic puree & tikka curry powder
- ½ tsp chili powder optional
- salt & pepper (as per taste)

Directions

- Prepare the butternut squash, onion, and carrots by peeling and dicing them. Add all of the ingredients to the slow cooker except garam masala. Mix your vegetables well with your hands so that the dry seasonings are well rubbed into the vegetables.
- Place your chicken breasts on top of the veggies and season with the remainder of the garam masala. Place the lid on your slow cooker and cook for 4 hours on high for shredded chicken or 3 hours on high for cubed chicken.
- Then remove the chicken with a spatula and put it to one side. Blend the vegetables until smooth. Either dice or shred the chicken and stir it into the butter chicken curry sauce.
- Serve with your favorite sides like collards or mustard greens.

Nutrition Info

Calories: 198kcal

Carbohydrates: 17g

Protein: 26g

Fat: 3g

Sugar: 16g

Fiber: 14g

48. Healthy Fish Stew

Preparation Time:	Cooking Time:	Serving
10 Minutes	25 Minutes	2

Ingredients

- 2 skinless pollock fillets (about 1 cup)
- 3 oz. raw shelled king prawns
- 2 leeks, thinly sliced
- 2 tbsp olive oil
- 2 celery sticks, diced
- 1 tsp fennel seeds
- 1 large carrot, diced
- 14 oz chopped tomatoes
- 2 garlic cloves, finely chopped
- 2 cups hot fish stock, heated to a simmer

Directions

- In a large pan, heat the oil, then add the fennel seeds, carrots, celery, and garlic and simmer for 5 minutes, or until softened. Season with salt and pepper, then add the leeks, tomatoes, and stock. Bring to a boil, then lower to low heat and cover for 15-20 minutes, or until the veggies are soft and the sauce has thickened and reduced slightly.
- Add the fish, scatter over the prawns and cook for 2 mins more until lightly cooked. Ladle into bowls and serve with a spoon.

Nutrition Info

Calories: 342kcal

Carbohydrates: 20g

Protein: 41g

Fat: 8g

Sugars: 13g

Fibers: 7g

49. Marinated Steak Bites

Preparation Time:	**Cooking Time:**	**Serving**
10 Minutes	4 Minutes	4

Ingredients

- 16 oz top sirloin or ribeye steak cut into 1-inch cubes
- Marinade
- 1/2 cup soy sauce
- 1/3 cup olive oil
- 1/8 cup Worcestershire sauce
- 1 tsp garlic minced
- 2 tbsp dried basil
- 1 tbsp dried parsley
- 1 tsp pepper
- 1 tsp salt

Directions

- Place all ingredients except the steak in a large bowl or zip-lock bag. Stir to combine.
- Drop in steak pieces and seal (or cover bowl) for about 30 minutes.
- Heat a large skillet to medium-high heat. Remove steak pieces from the marinade and place in a hot skillet. Discard the remaining marinade.
- Cook for 1 minute then flip each piece and cook for an additional minute. That is for medium steaks, so cook longer if you prefer yours well done. Serve hot!

Nutrition Info

Calories: 389kcal

Carbohydrates: 6g

Protein: 31g

Fat: 22g

50. Stuffed Tuna Steak

Preparation Time:	Cooking Time:	Serving
10 Minutes	25 Minutes	2

Ingredients

- 1 (8-ounce) tuna steak (about 2 inches thick)
- 1 tbsp olive oil
- 1 tbsp fresh lemon juice
- ½ cup fresh spinach, chopped
- 1 tsp olive oil
- 1 clove of garlic, minced
- ½ cup crumbled feta

Directions

- Lightly oil the grate of an outside grill and preheat it to high heat. Make a slit in the steak to make a pocket that is only open on one side. Brush 1 tbsp olive oil and 1 tbsp lemon juice over both sides of the fish in a cup. Place aside.
- In a small skillet, heat 2 tsp olive oil, and garlic over medium heat. Cook spinach in oil until wilted. Remove from heat, and stuff into a pocket. Place the feta in a pocket over the spinach. Arrange fish on the grill, and cook for 8 minutes. Turn over, and continue cooking until cooked through. Serve and enjoy!

Nutrition Info

Calories: 307kcal

Carbohydrates: 4g

Protein: 29g

Fat: 11.5g

Sugars: 1.2g

Fiber: 0.7g

51. Teriyaki Chicken

Preparation Time:	Cooking Time:	Serving
10 Minutes	20 Minutes	2

Ingredients

- 1 cup shredded chicken
- 1 tbsp minced ginger
- 4 tbsp teriyaki sauce
- 1 tsp avocado or coconut oil
- 1 cup of brown rice
- 2 cups broccoli
- 1 whole pineapple
- 1 tbsp minced garlic
- 2 tbsp sliced green onions
- sesame seeds and red pepper flakes for garnish

Directions

- Cut the pineapple in half (a long way). Scoop out the insides and save them as extras. Make sure to drain out most of the juice from the inside of these pineapple halves as they will serve as the bowl for your food. Gather the rest of the ingredients.
- Then, in a skillet, stir-fry the Chicken in the avocado oil with the garlic, teriyaki sauce, and ground ginger.
- Heat the brown rice and broccoli in the microwave or stir-fry into the skillet with the chicken. Then plate your bowl! Put some sesame seeds, green onion, and red pepper flakes on top.

Nutrition Info

Calories: 497kcal

Carbohydrates: 35g

Protein: 31g

Fat: 9g

Sugars: 28g

Fiber: 11g

52. Halibut with Brussels Sprouts

Preparation Time:	**Cooking Time:**	**Serving**
5 Minutes	20 Minutes	4

Ingredients

- 10 ounces fresh Brussels sprouts, halved
- 4 (4 to 6 ounces each) halibut fillets
- 1 tsp minced fresh ginger root
- 5 garlic cloves, sliced lengthwise
- ¼ to ¾ tsp salt, divided
- 4 tbsp lemon juice
- ¼ tsp pepper
- ½ cup water
- 2 tbsp canola oil
- 2 tbsp sesame oil
- 2 tbsp soy sauce
- Lemon slices, optional
- red pepper flakes, crushed

Directions

- Brush lemon juice over halibut fillets. Sprinkle with minced ginger, 1/4 tsp salt and pepper. Place fish on an oiled grill rack, skin side down. Grill, covered, over medium heat (or broil 6 in. from heat) until fish just begins to flake easily with a fork, 6-8 minutes.
- In a large skillet, bring water to a boil over medium-high heat. Add Brussels sprouts, pepper flakes and, if desired, remaining salt. Cook, covered, until tender, 5-7 minutes. Meanwhile, in a small skillet, heat oil over medium heat. Add garlic; cook until golden brown. Drain on paper towels.
- Drizzle sesame oil and soy sauce over halibut. Serve with Brussels sprouts; sprinkle with fried garlic. Serve with lemon slices, if desired.

Nutrition Info

Calories: 235kcal

Carbohydrates:7g

Protein: 26g

Fat: 13g

Sugars: 3g

Fiber: 5g

53. Salmon with Veggies

Preparation Time:	Cooking Time:	Serving
10 Minutes	25 Minutes	4

Ingredients

- ½ tsp. paprika
- 1 lb. salmon
- ½ sweet potato
- 2 cups of cauliflower
- ½ tsp. ground ginger
- 2 tbsp. olive oil
- 1 tbsp. soy sauce
- ½ tsp. garlic powder
- ½ tsp. cumin
- 1 cup cooked and diced beets
- 4 lemon wedges
- handful of parsley
- salt and pepper, to taste

Directions

- Firstly, preheat the oven to 400F (200C). Combine 1 tbsp. olive oil, garlic, and ginger. Toss in the cauliflower to cover it with the mixture and spread it on baking sheets.
- Get combine 1 tbsp olive oil with cumin and paprika. Cut sweet potatoes into cubes, cover them in the mixture of oil, and spread them on baking sheets. Roast in the oven for 25-30 minutes and stir midway.
- Sprinkle salmon with salt and pepper. Add another tbsp of olive oil to the frying pan, fry the salmon for a minute and add soy sauce.
- Cook the salmon for 1-2 minutes and flip the salmon, so it's skin down. Then, cook for another 3-5 minutes until the salmon is fully cooked.
- Then dice the beetroots and chop parsley. Divide salmon and vegetables between glass containers and top up with fresh parsley as well as lemon wedges.

Nutrition Info

Calories: 683kcal

Carbohydrates: 33g

Protein: 42g

Fat: 9g

Sugars: 8grams

Fibers: 7grams

54. Pesto-Crusted Cod

Preparation Time:	Cooking Time:	Serving
15 Minutes	10 Minutes	2

Ingredients

- a large pack of basil leaves only
- 3 tbsp olive oil
- 4 garlic cloves, 2 wholes, 2 crushed
- 2 red chilies, finely chopped
- 3-4 pine nuts
- 1 lemon
- 2 cod fillets
- 2 large tomatoes, roughly chopped
- 1 cup cooked lentils

Directions

- First, make the pesto. In a food processor, pulse the basil, whole garlic cloves, pine nuts, the juice of half the lemon and some seasoning, gradually adding most of the oil. Taste and adjust the seasoning.
- Then heat oven to 180C/160C fan/ gas 4 and line a roasting tin with foil. Season the cod on both sides and coat each fillet in the pesto. Cook for 8-10 mints until a crust has formed and the cod is cooked through.
- Heat the remaining oil in a small saucepan. Add the crushed garlic and the chilies, and cook for a couple of mints to release the flavor. Add the tomatoes and cook for 1 min more.
- Tip in the lentils, squeeze over the other half of the lemon, then season. Cook until piping hot. Serve with the pesto cod and enjoy!

Nutrition Info

Calories: 624kcal

Carbohydrates: 27g

Protein: 36g

Fat: 21g

Sugars: 8g

Fibers: 11g

55. Steak Fajita Bowls

Preparation Time:	**Cooking Time:**	**Serving**
5 Minutes	15 Minutes	2-4

Ingredients

- 9 oz. of steak
- 2 cups of bell peppers
- 2 cups of brown rice
- 4-5 green leaf lettuce
- ½ cup of white corn
- 1 yellow onion
- a handful of fresh cilantros
- ½ tsp. red pepper flakes
- jalapenos (optional)
- avocado (optional)

Directions

- Firstly, cut the onion and portion out two cups of bell peppers. Cut the steak into strips.
- Heat a skillet and then spray with nonstick spray. Grill the steak and vegetables until cooked.
- In the microwave, heat two cups of Trifecta brown rice. (For best results, place a wet paper towel on top of the bowl of rice before heating)
- Drain a can of corn and rinse off. On a plate, portion out the base layer of rice, steak, and fajita veggies. Put some lettuce, cabbage, corn, jalapenos, and red pepper flakes on top.

Nutrition Info

Calories: 429kcal

Carbohydrates: 34g

Protein: 35g

Fat: 9g

Sugar: 8g

Fiber: 16g

56. Honey-Chili Meatloaf

Preparation Time:	**Cooking Time:**	**Serving**
5 Minutes	15 Minutes	4

Ingredients

For the meatloaf:

- 7oz turkey patties
- green onions
- garlic
- 1 egg
- ½ cup of panko bread crumbs
- ¼ cup of pineapple (not for the inside of the meatloaf)

For the sauce:

- ¼ cup of chili sauce
- 3 minced garlic gloves
- 3 tbsp. rice vinegar
- 3 tbsp. soy sauce
- 3 tbsp. honey
- ½ tsp. toasted sesame oil

Directions

- Take a large bowl; mix all of the ingredients for the turkey meatloaf. Roll meatloaf into 1-inch balls. Place off to the side when rolled.
- Next heat up a skillet over medium. Grill the turkey meatloaf on all sides, until each side is slightly browned. (Cover the skillet for 1-2 minutes to cook the inside of the meatloaf before removing from heat).
- Then in a small bowl, mix all of the ingredients for the sauce. Dip the cooked meatloaf into the sauce until thoroughly glazed in the sauce. Pair the meatloaf with brown rice. Add in the pineapple. Top with sesame seeds and green onions and mustard greens.
- Serve with lime for additional flavor.

Nutrition Info

Calories: 450kcal

Carbohydrates: 20g

Protein: 31g

Fat: 12g

Sugars: 18g

Fiber: 3g

57. Low Carb Sage-Rubbed Salmon

Preparation Time:	**Cooking Time:**	**Serving**
5 Minutes	15 Minutes	6

Ingredients

- 1-1/2 pounds skin-on salmon fillet
- 2 tbsp minced fresh sage
- 1 tsp garlic powder
- 1 tsp kosher salt
- 1 tsp freshly ground pepper
- 2 tbsp olive oil

Directions

- Preheat oven to 375°. Mix fresh sage, garlic powder, salt and pepper. Then rub it onto the flesh side of the salmon. Cut into 6 portions.
- In a large cast-iron skillet, heat oil over medium heat. Add salmon, skin side down; cook for 5 minutes. Transfer skillet to oven; bake just until fish flakes easily with a fork, about 10 minutes. Serve and enjoy!

Nutrition Info

Calories: 220kcal

Carbohydrates: 1g

Protein: 21g

Fat: 9g

58. Ginger Salmon

Preparation Time:	Cooking Time:	Serving
5 Minutes	25 Minutes	2

Ingredients

- 1/4 cup lemon juice
- 2 tbsp rice vinegar
- 3 garlic cloves, minced
- 2 tsp. minced fresh gingerroot
- 2 tsp. honey
- 1/8 tsp salt
- 1/8 tsp pepper
- 2 salmon fillets (6 oz each)
- 1 medium lemon, thinly sliced

Green beans:

- 1/2-pound fresh green beans, trimmed
- 2 tbsp water
- 2 tsp. olive oil
- 1/2 cup finely chopped onion
- 3 garlic cloves, minced
- 1/8 tsp salt

Directions

- Preheat oven to 325°F. Mix the first 7 ingredients.
- Place each salmon fillet on an 18x12-in. piece of heavy-duty foil; fold up the edges of the foil to create a rim around the fish. Spoon lemon juice mixture over salmon; top with lemon slices. Carefully fold the foil around the fish, sealing it tightly.
- Place packets in a 15x10x1-in. pan. Bake until fish just begins to flake easily with a fork, 15-20 minutes. Open the foil carefully to allow steam to escape.
- Meanwhile, place green beans, water and oil in a large skillet; bring to a boil. Reduce heat; simmer, covered, for 5 minutes. Stir in remaining ingredients; cook, uncovered, until beans are crisp-tender, stirring occasionally. Serve with salmon.

Nutrition Info

Calories: 357kcal

Carbohydrates: 27g

Protein: 33g

Fat: 15g

Sugar: 9g

Fiber 5g

59. Orange Chicken and Brown Rice

Preparation Time:	**Cooking Time:**	**Serving**
5 Minutes	20 Minutes	4

Ingredients

- 1 lb. lean ground chicken
- 1-1/2 cups sliced fresh mushrooms
- 1 medium onion, chopped
- 2 garlic cloves, minced
- 1 tsp minced fresh gingerroot
- 2 tbsp reduced-sodium soy sauce
- 1 package (14 oz) coleslaw mix
- 1 tbsp sesame oil
- 2 cups hot cooked brown rice
- ½ cup sweet-and-sour sauce

Directions

- In a large cast-iron or other heavy skillet, cook and crumble chicken with mushrooms, onion, garlic and ginger over medium-high heat until no longer pink, 6-8 minutes; drain. Stir in soy sauce.
- Add coleslaw mix; cook and stir until wilted, 3-4 minutes. Stir in sesame oil. Serve 1-1/4 cups of chicken mixture with rice and sweet-and-sour sauce.

Nutrition Info

Calories: 391kcal

Carbohydrates: 27g

Protein: 30g

Fat: 11g

Sugars: 20g

Fiber: 11g

60. Herbed Balsamic Chicken

Preparation Time:	Cooking Time:	Serving
5 Minutes	20 Minutes	6

Ingredients

- ½ cup balsamic vinegar
- 3 tbsp extra virgin olive oil
- 1 tbsp fresh basil, minced
- 1 tbsp fresh chives, minced
- 2 tsp. grated lemon zest
- 1 garlic clove, minced
- 3/4 tsp salt
- 1/4 tsp pepper
- 6 boneless skinless chicken thighs (1-1/2 pounds)

Directions

- Whisk together all ingredients except chicken. In a bowl, toss chicken with 1/3 cup vinegar mixture; let stand 10 minutes.
- Grill chicken, covered, over medium heat or broil 4 in. from heat until a thermometer reads 338°F, 6-8 minutes per side. Drizzle with the remaining vinegar mixture before serving.

Nutrition Info

Calories: 324kcal

Carbohydrates: 6g

Protein: 21g

Fat: 15g

61. Mexican Tuna Salad with Avocado

Preparation Time:	Cooking Time:	Serving
20 Minutes	0 Minutes	4

Ingredients

- 1 tbsp lime juice
- 1 tbsp extra virgin olive oil
- ½ tsp paprika
- 12 ounces Tuna
- 1/2 cup red pepper, diced
- 15-ounce can of black beans rinsed and drained
- 1/2 tsp cumin
- 1 lime zested
- 2 avocados, cubed
- 1/2 - 1 cup cilantro, chopped
- 1/4 - ½ small red onion, diced
- 1 - 2 tsp chopped jalapeno
- 1 tsp salt

Directions

- In a small bowl combine lime juice, olive oil and paprika. Mix until smooth.
- In a large bowl combine the remaining ingredients and mix. Top with the dressing.

Nutrition Info

Calories: 470kcal

Carbohydrates: 29g

Protein: 33g

Fat: 25g

Sugar: 2.2g

Fiber: 16g

62. Vegan Fall Farro Protein Bowl

Preparation Time:	Cooking Time:	Serving
15 Minutes	30 Minutes	4

Ingredients

- ½ cup sweet potatoes, diced
- ½ cup carrots, diced
- 2 tsp organic cooking oil, divided
- 15-ounce can of chickpeas, drained and rinsed
- 4 ounces smoky tempeh strips (1/2 package, typically)
- 2 ½ cups water
- 1 cup uncooked farro
- salt & pepper
- 2 cups mixed greens
- ½ cup hummus
- ¼ cup roasted almonds
- 4 lemon wedges

Directions

- Preheat oven to 375°F, and get a large baking sheet out.
- In a mixing bowl, toss sweet potatoes and carrots with 1 tsp cooking oil, and a pinch of salt & pepper. Spread out in a single layer, on a third of the baking sheet.
- In the same mixing bowl, toss the chickpeas with the remaining 1 tsp of oil, a pinch of salt and 1/8 tsp black pepper, until coated. Spread out in a single layer on the second third of the baking sheet. Place tempeh strips on the remaining third, and roast the three for 30 minutes. Flip tempeh strips, and shuffle around the sweet potatoes and chickpeas (while keeping them separate), for 15 minutes.
- While those are roasting, place water, farro grains and a hefty pinch of salt into a small pot over medium heat. Cover, bring to a boil, then reduce to medium-low, cooking for 20-25 minutes or until the grains are chewy but soft.
- Once the farro is done, divide it and the greens between two bowls. When the potatoes, chickpeas, and tempeh are roasted, season with salt, if necessary, then divide amongst the two bowls, finishing with hummus, almonds and lemon wedges (for squeezing over). Serve while warm, and enjoy!

Nutrition Info

Calories: 423kcal

Carbohydrates: 42g

Protein: 24g

Fat: 15g

Sugars: 8g

Fiber: 15g

63. Protein Monster Vegan Enchiladas

Preparation Time:	**Cooking Time:**	**Serving**
25 Minutes	25 Minutes	6

Ingredients

- 1 yellow onion
- 1 red bell pepper
- 15 oz. can of black beans
- 15 oz. can garbanzo beans (chickpeas)
- 1/2 cup hemp hearts
- 1/3 cup nutritional yeast
- 3 Roma tomatoes
- 2 tsp. ground cumin
- 1 tsp. smoked paprika
- 6 large tortillas
- 1 batch of homemade enchilada sauce (or your favorite)

Directions

- Make the enchilada sauce and set aside. (Or skip this step if using your sauce.)
- Preheat oven to 350°F (176°C). Dice onion and bell pepper. In a large skillet over medium heat, sauté onion and bell pepper for about 8 minutes. Meanwhile, dice tomatoes. Rinse and drain beans.
- When onions are translucent, reduce heat. Add cumin, paprika, tomatoes, nutritional yeast, hemp hearts, and both beans (rinsed and drained). Stir well. Heat for 4-5 minutes then set aside.
- In a lightly sprayed 9"×13" baking dish, cover the bottom with a thin layer of enchilada sauce. Distribute the bean mixture in the center of the tortillas. Roll up, tucking in both ends.
- Place all 6 rolled enchiladas in the baking dish and top with the remaining sauce. Bake for about 25 minutes. Serve topped with avocado, cilantro, additional hemp hearts, nutritional yeast, etc.

Nutrition Info

Calories: 413kcal

Carbohydrates: 42g

Protein: 27g

Fat: 19g

Sugars: 7g

Fiber: 15g

64. Asian Quinoa Bowls with Baked Tofu

Preparation Time:	Cooking Time:	Serving
5 Minutes	30 Minutes	6

Ingredients

- 1 cup uncooked quinoa
- 1 tsp ground ginger
- 3 tsp tamari divided
- 1 cup water
- 1 ¼ cups almond breeze almond milk coconut milk blend, divided
- 1/4 cup peanut butter
- juice of 1 lime
- 1 tsp sriracha
- 1 block extra firm tofu, cubed
- 2 cups cabbage, shredded
- 2 cups carrots, shredded
- 1 bunch of scallion, sliced
- ¼ cup cilantro, chopped
- sesame seeds to garnish optional

Directions

- Add quinoa, ginger, 1 tsp tamari, water and 1 cup of almond milk coconut milk blend into a small saucepan. Bring mixture to a boil, cover and reduce to a simmer for 15 minutes. Once the liquid has been absorbed, set aside until ready to serve.
- While the quinoa is cooking, preheat the oven to 400°F. Grease a baking sheet and set aside. In a small bowl, whisk together peanut butter, remaining 1/4 cup of almond milk coconut milk blend, remaining 2 tsp of tamari, lime juice and hot sauce. Continue to whisk until smooth and pourable (add a splash more almond milk as needed).
- Add tofu to a mixing bowl and toss with half of the peanut dressing. Transfer the tofu to the greased baking sheet and bake for 30 minutes until crispy, flipping halfway through.
- Once the tofu is done, assemble your bowls. Divide the quinoa, tofu, cabbage, carrots and scallions evenly among 4 bowls. Drizzle each with the remaining dressing and sprinkle with cilantro and sesame seeds. Enjoy immediately!

Nutrition Info

Calories: 484kcal

Carbohydrates: 43g

Protein: 34g

Fat: 31g

Sugars: 12g

Fiber: 14g

65. Chicken Parmesan Zucchini Boats Recipe

Preparation Time:	Cooking Time:	Serving
10 Minutes	45 Minutes	4

Ingredients

- 4 medium zucchinis about 1 ¾ pounds
- 1 lb. ground chicken
- 1/4 tsp. salt
- 1/4 tsp. ground black pepper
- 2 garlic cloves, minced
- 1 cup pasta sauce
- 1/4 cup grated parmesan cheese
- 1/2 cup mozzarella cheese, shredded
- Optional: sliced fresh basil for topping

Directions

- Preheat oven to 400 degrees F. Spray a 9x13-inch baking dish with cooking spray. Place a large non-stick skillet over medium-high heat. Add the chicken and break it apart with a spoon. Add the salt and pepper. Cook for 8 to 10 minutes, until chicken, is cooked through. Stir occasionally and break down the chicken into small chunks.
- Reduce the heat to low. Add the garlic to the chicken. Cook for 1 minute stirring often. Add the pasta sauce. Cook for 3 minutes, stirring occasionally.
- As the chicken cooks, cut the zucchini in half, lengthwise. Use a spoon to scoop the seeds and center out of each zucchini half, leaving a ¼ inch thick zucchini boat.
- Place the zucchini in the baking dish cut-side up. Spoon the chicken mixture into the zucchini boats. Press the mixture down into the zucchini using the back of the spoon.
- Sprinkle the zucchini evenly with the parmesan, then the mozzarella cheese. Cover the baking dish with foil. Bake for 35 minutes. Sprinkle with fresh basil and serve.

Nutrition Info

Calories: 332kcal

Carbohydrates: 13g

Protein: 38.2g

Fat: 17.8g

Sugars: 7g

Fibers: 4g

66. Tempeh Vegetarian Chili

Preparation Time:	Cooking Time:	Serving
5 Minutes	25 Minutes	6

Ingredients

- 2 tbsp olive oil
- 1 (8-oz) package of tempeh, roughly grated
- 1 medium white onion, diced
- 1 red bell pepper, diced
- 1 stalk celery, diced
- 2 cloves garlic, minced
- 3/4 cup tomato sauce
- 1 (15-oz) can of kidney beans, drained
- 1 (15-oz) can of black beans, drained
- 1 cup water
- 1 tsp each cumin and salt
- 1/4 tsp each chili powder and crushed red pepper flakes
- To serve: chopped green onions, plain Greek yogurt

Directions

- Brown Tempeh: Heat oil over medium/high heat in a large pot. Add tempeh and cook until lightly browned about 5 minutes. It's okay if some of it sticks to the bottom of the pan. It will come off when you add the liquids.
- Add Flavor Makers: Add onion, bell pepper, celery, and garlic, continuing to cook until veggies are a bit soft, about 5 minutes.
- Cook Everything: Add the remaining ingredients, reduce heat to medium, and cook until warm and the flavors have blended about 15 minutes. Taste and adjust seasonings as needed. Top with green onions and serve.

Nutrition Info

Calories: 422kcal

Carbohydrates: 44g

Protein: 30g

Fat: 22g

Sugars: 6g

Fiber: 15g

High Protein Desserts

67. Keto Peanut Butter Cookies

Preparation Time:	Cooking Time:	Serving
5 Minutes	15 Minutes	24

Ingredients

- 1 cup (128g) salted peanut butter
- ¼ cup (32g) almond flour
- ½ cup (64g) low-calorie sweetener (like stevia)
- 1 egg
- 1 tsp vanilla extract

Directions

- Preheat the oven to 350 F and line a baking sheet. Add all ingredients to a bowl and mix well. Using a spoon, scoop between 1-1.5 tbsp of dough and form it into a small ball and drop it onto the lined baking sheet.
- Repeat until the rest of the dough has been used up. You may need 2 baking trays. Make sure each cookie ball is about 1.5 inches away from the others.
- Using a fork, press down on the cookie to flatten it. Repeat in the opposite direction so you end up with crisscross marks. Continue till all the cookies are flattened.
- Bake in the preheated oven for 10-14 minutes or until the edges of the cookies are browning. Transfer the cookie sheet to a cooling rack and let them cool before removing them (as they are fragile and will break if you try and remove them when hot).

Nutrition Info

Calories: 72kcal

Carbohydrates: 2g

Protein: 4g

Fat: 4g

Sugars: 1g

Fiber: 3g

68. Pumpkin Spice Protein Balls

Preparation Time:	Cooking Time:	Serving
10 Minutes	0 Minutes	14

Ingredients

- ¾ cup peanut butter (187g)
- ½ cup pitted soft dates, packed (85g)
- ¼ cup protein powder, vanilla or unflavored (34g)
- ¼ cup chia seeds (40g)
- ⅓ cup oat flour (45g)
- 2 tsp pumpkin pie spice
- ¼ tsp salt

Directions

- Add all the ingredients into a food processor and blend until the ingredients form a cookie dough-like consistency.
- Scoop out 1 heaping tbsp of the mixture and roll them into balls. I was able to make 14 balls that weighed around 1oz (28g) each.
- Place them into a parchment-lined tray or container.
- Optional step: drizzle on some melted chocolate and top with hemp seeds (or crushed nuts/seeds of choice).
- Place them into the fridge or freezer to firm up for at least 30 minutes.

Nutrition Info

Calories: 132kcal

Carbohydrates: 11g

Protein: 8g

Fat: 5.4g

Sugars: 3g

Fiber: 4g

69. Vegan Protein Muffins

Preparation Time:	Cooking Time:	Serving
10 Minutes	20 Minutes	10

Ingredients

- 2 flax eggs (2 tbsp ground flaxseed + 5 tbsp water)
- 1 ¼ cups dairy-free yogurt, unsweetened
- 2 medium bananas, very ripe
- 2 cups rolled oats
- ⅓ cup Protein Powder, vanilla flavor
- ¼ cup maple syrup
- 1 tsp vanilla extract
- 1 ½ tsp baking powder
- ½ tsp baking soda
- ½ tsp sea salt

Directions

- Preheat oven to 400° degrees F. Lightly grease each slot of a standard muffin tin. Use paper liners to keep the recipe oil-free. Prepare flax eggs in a small bowl, by mixing the ground flax & water. Set aside about 10 minutes. It will thicken up and become gel-like.
- When the flax eggs are ready, add all the ingredients (except the toppings) into a high-powered blender or food processor. Blend until smooth, about 1-2 minutes. Scrape down sides as needed.
- Pour mixture into each slot about ¾ of the way full. Sprinkle each one with your favorite toppings. Bake for 15-18 minutes, until lightly golden brown. Insert a toothpick in the middle of a muffin or two. If it comes out mostly clean, they are done.
- Let muffins cool for 10 minutes in the pan before transferring them to a cooling rack, then cool for another 10-15 minutes. Enjoy!

Nutrition Info

Calories: 137kcal

Carbohydrates: 24g

Protein: 13g

Fat: 1g

Sugars: 65g

Fiber: 25g

70. High Protein Brownie

Preparation Time:	Cooking Time:	Serving
5 Minutes	5 Minutes	4

Ingredients

- 2 large egg whites
- ½ cup chocolate protein powder
- ¼ cup applesauce
- 3 tbsp unsweetened cocoa powder
- ½ cup powdered peanut butter
- 4 tsp creamy peanut butter

optional:

- dark chocolate chips

Directions

- In a mixing bowl, whisk together the egg whites, cocoa powder, applesauce, protein powder and powdered peanut butter until creamy and smooth.
- Divide into 4 ramekins and microwave for 1 to 2 minutes, or until brownie is set. Top each with a tsp of peanut butter and any additional toppings.

Nutrition Info

Calories: 96kcal

Carbohydrates: 6.6g

Protein: 11g

Fat: 2.6g

Sugars: 5g

Fiber: 7g

71. Chocolate Protein Pudding

Preparation Time:	Cooking Time:	Serving
5 Minutes	0 Minutes	1

Ingredients

- 1 serving of vegan chocolate protein powder, vegan
- 2 tbsp. cacao powder
- 3/4-1 cup milk, cold
- 1 tbsp. almond butter or coconut butter

Directions

- Combine the protein powder, cacao powder and milk in a bowl. Stir well until most of the lumps are fully removed. Start with 3/4 cup of dairy-free milk and add a little at a time so it doesn't get too runny.
- Once the lumps are gone, add the creamy almond butter or melted coconut butter and stir well until you have a pudding consistency. Refrigerate for up to 8 hours or serve immediately.

Nutrition Info

Calories: 234kcal

Carbohydrates: 17g

Protein: 21g

Fat: 13g

Sugars: 7g

Fiber: 6g

72. Cinnamon Swirl Protein Cake

Preparation Time:	**Cooking Time:**	**Serving**
5 Minutes	25 Minutes	1

Ingredients

- ¼ cup oats
- 1 egg white
- 1 scoop vanilla protein powder
- 2 tsp stevia
- ½ tbsp cinnamon
- ⅓ cup water

Directions

- Preheat the oven to 325 F (165 C). Blend the oats, egg white, and water until the consistency is smooth. Pour the mixture into a bowl. Whisk it together with the protein powder and 1 tsp. Stevia. The mixture should be like a thick pancake batter.
- Pour half of the batter into a small (about 4.5 inches across) nonstick pan and sprinkle with two-thirds of the cinnamon plus 1 tsp. Stevia. Pour the remaining batter and sprinkle with the rest of the cinnamon.
- Pull a knife through the batter a few times to slightly mix in the cinnamon and Stevia. Bake for 25 minutes and let it rest for a few minutes before serving.

Nutrition Info

Calories: 217kcal

Carbohydrates: 17g

Protein: 31g

Fat: 2g

Sugars: 2.5g

Fiber: 2g

73. High Protein Berry Crumble

Preparation Time:	Cooking Time:	Serving
5 Minutes	15 Minutes	1

Ingredients

- 1 cup fresh or frozen raspberries or mixed berries
- 1 tsp Stevia
- 1 scoop vanilla protein powder
- ¼ cup oats
- 2 tbsp lemon juice
- 10 almonds

Directions

- Preheat oven to 350F (180C). Place berries in a small Pyrex oven dish and sprinkle a little Stevia on top. Mix the protein powder, oats, and lemon juice. It will be fairly dry. Chop the almonds into small pieces and mix them with the crumble.
- Spread the crumble on top of the berries. Bake for 15 min, then set the oven to broil and bake the crumble for another 1-2 minutes until the top is slightly golden.
- Take out of the oven and allow to cool slightly before serving.

Nutrition Info

Calories: 320kcal

Carbohydrates: 34g

Protein: 29g

Fat: 8g

Sugars: 7.5g

Fiber: 8g

74. Protein Brownie Bites

Preparation Time:	Cooking Time:	Serving
5 Minutes	15 Minutes	12

Ingredients

- 1 cup Pumpkin puree or sweet potato or banana
- ½ cup almond butter or peanut butter, cashew butter, or a nut butter alternative
- ¼ cup cocoa powder
- 1-2 scoops protein powder
- 1 serving liquid stevia

Directions

- Preheat the oven to 350°F (180°C) and line a mini muffin tin with mini muffin liners- For smaller brownie bites, you'll need at least 15. Ensure each muffin tin in greased generously. In a high-speed blender or mixing bowl, combine all your ingredients and blend/mix until smooth.
- Pour brownie mixture into each muffin tin, filling until just full. As there is no baking powder needed, they generally won't rise.
- Bake for 12-15 minutes, or until a skewer/toothpick comes out just clean. Allow cooling in the muffin tin completely. For best results, refrigerate once cooled for several hours.

Nutrition Info

Calories: 95kcal

Carbohydrates: 5g

Protein: 8g

Fat: 4g

Sugars: 1g

Fiber: 18g

75. Healthy Strawberry Protein Fluff

Preparation Time:	**Cooking Time:**	**Serving**
15 Minutes	0 Minutes	3

Ingredients

- 2½ cups (210g) frozen strawberries
- ½ cup unsweetened vanilla almond milk
- ½ tsp vanilla crème-flavored stevia extract
- ⅓ cup (30g) unflavored casein protein powder
- ¾ tsp xanthan gum

Directions

- In a food processor, add the frozen strawberries, almond milk, and stevia extract. Puree until almost completely smooth.
- In a small bowl, whisk together the protein powder and xanthan gum. Dump this into the processor and blend again. After about 10 seconds, scrape down the sides of the processor to catch any powder that is flung up, then blend again.
- Blend for ~1 full minute, or until the mixture doubles in volume and turns a nice pink color. Serve immediately.

Nutrition Info

Calories: 65kcal

Carbohydrates: 5g

Protein: 9g

Fat: 0.5g

Sugars: 13g

Fiber: 8g

76. Chocolate Peanut Butter Frozen Yogurt Bark

Preparation Time:	Cooking Time:	Serving
10 Minutes	0 Minutes	6

Ingredients

- ½ cup plain whole-milk Greek or regular vanilla yogurt
- 3 tbsp creamy salted peanut butter
- 1–2 tsp honey or agave (optional)
- 2 tbsp mini chocolate chips

Directions

- Combine the yogurt, 2 tbsp of peanut butter, and honey (if using) until completely mixed.
- Spread the yogurt mixture into an even layer on parchment paper, until it's about 4 inches by 6 inches, or ½ inch thick.
- Sprinkle with chocolate chips and drizzle the remaining peanut butter on too. Transfer to the freezer and let chill for 1 hour or until completely frozen.
- Break into small pieces and store in an airtight container in the freezer.

Nutrition Info

Calories: 108kcal

Carbohydrates: 5g

Protein: 6g

Fat: 7.3g

Sugars: 6g

Fiber: 2g

High Protein Pre-Workouts

77. Blackberry Layered Smoothie

Preparation Time:	**Cooking Time:**	**Serving**
10 Minutes	0 Minutes	3

Ingredients

Bottom Layer

- 1 cup low-fat plain yogurt
- Juice from ½ lime
- 1 ripe avocado peeled and pit removed
- 1 tsp honey
- 2 scoop protein powder

Top Layer

- 1 1/3 cups wild blackberry frozen
- ¼ cup peanut butter
- 1 cup low-fat plain yogurt
- 1/3 cup milk

Directions

- Bottom Layer: Blend the following: 1 ripe avocado, peeled and pit removed 1 cup (250 mL) low-fat plain yogurt Juice from 1/2 lime 3 tbsp (45 ml) honey
- Divide equally among four glasses. Set aside while making the top layer.
- Top Layer: Blend the following: 1 1/3 cup (325 ml) wild blackberries, frozen 1/4 cup (60 ml) peanut butter, 1 cup (250 ml) low-fat plain yogurt, 1/3 cup (75 ml) 1% milk. Pour into glasses, overtop avocado blend. Enjoy!

Nutrition Info

Calories: 308kcal

Carbohydrates: 17g

Protein: 19g

Fat: 18g

Sugars: 15g

Fiber: 20g

78. Banana Pear Smoothie

Preparation Time:	Cooking Time:	Serving
5 Minutes	0 Minutes	2

Ingredients

- 2 ripe pears, pitted and coarsely chopped
- 1 tsp ginger root peeled and coarsely chopped
- 1 banana
- 1 cup skim milk
- 1 scoop protein powder
- handful ice
- Sprinkle cinnamon on top

Directions

- Blend all ingredients. Enjoy!

Nutrition Info

Calories: 189kcal

Carbohydrates: 32g

Protein: 26g

Fat: 1g

Sugars: 23g

Fiber:8g

79. Banana-Walnut Bliss

Preparation Time:	**Cooking Time:**	**Serving**
5 Minutes	0 Minutes	2

Ingredients

- 2 cups skim milk
- 1 large banana
- 1 tbsp honey
- 1/4 tsp vanilla extract
- 2 scoop protein powder
- a handful of walnut pieces (or 7 halves)

Directions

- Blend all ingredients. Enjoy!

Nutrition Info

Calories: 227kcal

Carbohydrates: 34g

Protein: 28g

Fat: 5g

Sugars: 23g

Fiber: 3g

80. Banana smoothies with cinnamon

Preparation Time:	Cooking Time:	Serving
5 Minutes	0 Minutes	1-2

Ingredients

- 1 ripe banana, peeled
- ½ cup frozen blueberries
- 1 tsp maple syrup
- 1 tsp cinnamon
- juice from ½ lemon
- 2 scoops protein powder
- 1/2 cup unsweetened almond or oat milk

Directions

- Add all ingredients to a blender and blend until completely smooth.
- Enjoy 30 minutes before working out for the best benefits. Enjoy!

Nutrition Info

Calories: 305kcal

Carbohydrates: 36g

Protein: 22g

Fat: 3g

Sugars: 22g

Fiber: 7g

81. Healthy Muscles Smoothie

Preparation Time:	Cooking Time:	Serving
5 Minutes	0 Minutes	1

Ingredients

- 1 cup spinach
- ½ cup coconut water
- ½ cup water
- ½ cup pineapple frozen
- ½ cup peach frozen
- ½ banana
- 1 tbsp coconut oil (optional)
- 1 scoop protein powder

Directions

- Blend the spinach, coconut water and water until smooth.
- Add the pineapple, peaches, banana and coconut oil, and blend again. Serve!

Nutrition Info

Calories: 272kcal

Carbohydrates: 32g

Protein: 24g

Fat: 15g

Sugars: 22g

Fiber: 8g

82. Vegan Blackberry Smoothie

Preparation Time:	**Cooking Time:**	**Serving**
10 Minutes	0 Minutes	1

Ingredients

- 1 ½ cup soy milk (or milk of choice)
- ½ cup blackberries (preferably frozen)
- ½ mango, diced
- 2 tbsp oats
- 1 tbsp pumpkin seeds
- 1 tbsp flax seeds
- 1 tsp almond butter
- 1 ½ tsp sugar
- 1-2 ice cubes
- ½ scoop protein powder

Directions

- Blend all the ingredients until creamy and fully incorporated. Serve!

Nutrition Info

Calories: 382kcal

Carbohydrates: 35g

Protein: 22g

Fat: 19g

Sugars: 18g

Fiber: 9g

83. Minty Pineapple and Spinach Smoothie

Preparation Time:	Cooking Time:	Serving
7 Minutes	0 Minutes	1

Ingredients

- 2 oz. pineapple chunks (preferably frozen)
- 1 small sprig of mint, fresh
- 5 oz Greek yogurt
- ¼ tsp vanilla extract
- 1.5 oz baby spinach
- 1 tbsp flax seeds
- 1 tbsp cashews
- 1.5 tsp maple syrup
- 2 tbsp rolled oats
- 1 ice cubes

Directions

- Add all the ingredients to the blender. 4oz pineapple chunks, 1 small sprig mint, fresh, 5oz Greek yogurt, ¼ tsp vanilla extract, 1.5oz baby spinach, 1 tbsp flax seed, 1 tbsp cashew, 1.5 tsp maple syrup, 2 tbsp rolled oats, 1 ice cube.
- Blend until fully incorporated and creamy. You shouldn't see the texture of the solids; everything should be as smooth as possible.
- Taste and add extra mint leaves if you want more mint flavor.

Nutrition Info

Calories: 438kcal

Carbohydrates: 31g

Protein: 21g

Fat: 14g

Sugars: 26g

Fiber: 9g

84. Avocado Spinach Smoothie

Preparation Time:	Cooking Time:	Serving
6 Minutes	0 Minutes	2

Ingredients

- 1 handful spinach
- 1 tbsp parsley, fresh
- ½ avocado
- 1 tsp cacao powder
- 1 tsp cinnamon
- ⅓ tsp sea salt
- 1 tbsp olive oil
- 1 tbsp walnuts (almonds are fine too)
- 1 tsp dark chocolate nibs
- 2 tsp coconut flakes
- ½ cup water
- ½ tsp maple syrup
- ½ cup soy milk
- 1 serving of protein powder

Directions

- Throw everything into a blender and blend for 60 seconds.
- 1 handful spinach, 1 tbsp parsley, fresh, ½ avocado, 1 tsp cacao powder, 1 tsp cinnamon, ⅓ tsp sea salt, 1 tbsp olive oil, 1 tbsp walnuts, 1 tsp dark chocolate nibs, 2 tsp coconut flakes, ½ cup water, ½ tsp maple syrup, ½ cup soy milk, 1 serving protein powder. Done.

Nutrition Info

Calories: 292kcal

Carbohydrates: 15g

Protein: 14g

Fat: 21g

Sugars: 5g

Fiber: 10g

85. Fruity Smoothie with Yogurt

Preparation Time:	**Cooking Time:**	**Serving**
5 Minutes	0 Minutes	2

Ingredients

- 1 ripe banana, peeled
- 1 cup strawberries frozen, chopped
- 1 cup mango frozen, chopped
- 1 cup natural Greek yogurt unsweetened

Directions

- Place the banana with the strawberry and mango pieces in a high-powered blender. Mix for 2 minutes, until no solid pieces remain.
- 1 ripe banana, 1 cup frozen, chopped, strawberries, 1 cup frozen, chopped, mango. Add the yogurt and mix for 30 seconds, until well combined.
- Pour 1 cup of natural Greek yogurt into a tall glass and decorate it with a few pieces of strawberries and a paper straw. Serve immediately!

Nutrition Info

Calories: 215kcal

Carbohydrates: 30g

Protein: 18g

Fat: 2g

Sugars: 36g

Fiber: 8g

86. Super Spinach Smoothie

Preparation Time:	**Cooking Time:**	**Serving**
3 Minutes	0 Minutes	1

Ingredients

- 1 medium banana
- 1 big handful of spinach
- 1 tbsp peanut butter
- 1 ¼ cup unsweetened soy milk (milk – almond, oat, coconut)

Directions

- Add 1 medium banana, 1 big handful of spinach, 1 tbsp peanut butter, and 1 ¼ cup unsweetened soy milk and blend!

Nutrition Info

Calories: 310kcal

Carbohydrates: 37g

Protein: 15g

Fat: 13g

Sugars: 16g

Fiber: 7g

87. Chocolate Peanut Butter Protein Smoothie

Preparation Time:	**Cooking Time:**	**Serving**
50 Minutes	Minutes	1

Ingredients

- 1 large banana, peeled, sliced, and frozen
- 3 tbsp unsweetened cocoa powder
- 6 oz Greek yogurt (flavored or unflavored)
- 3/4 cup skim milk
- 1 tbsp honey, maple syrup, or agave
- 1 tbsp peanut butter

Directions

- Make sure you have a strong, powerful blender that will blend up the frozen banana.
- Put all of the ingredients into the blender, in the order listed, and blend on high until thick and smooth.
- Start with only 2 tbsp of cocoa powder, blend, and then add 1 more for a stronger chocolate taste. You may need to stop and stir/scrape down the sides of the blender a few times. Drizzle the glass with 1 tsp of chocolate syrup (optional) and enjoy!

Nutrition Info

Calories: 225kcal

Carbohydrates: 31g

Protein: 28g

Fat: 5g

Sugars: 38g

Fiber: 9g

88. Banana And Almond Smoothie

Preparation Time:	Cooking Time:	Serving
5 Minutes	0 Minutes	1

Ingredients

- 1 banana
- 1 tsp almond butter
- 2 heaped tbsp oats
- 200 ml skimmed milk
- 1 scoop protein powder

Directions

- Put the frozen banana, almond butter (1 tsp), oats (2 heaped tbsp) and skimmed milk (200ml) into a blender. Blend until smooth. Serve.

Nutrition Info

Calories: 292kcal

Carbohydrates: 41g

Protein: 22g

Fat: 8g

Sugars: 24g

Fiber: 6g

89. Kiwi Banana Smoothie

Preparation Time:	Cooking Time:	Serving
3 Minutes	0 Minutes	2

Ingredients

- 2 kiwis
- 1 banana
- ¾ cup milk (soy, almond, coconut, etc.)
- ¾ cup low-fat yogurt
- 4 tbsp porridge oats
- 1 thumb ginger, fresh
- 1 scoop protein powder

Directions

- Add all the ingredients to the blender and blend well. Enjoy!

Nutrition Info

Calories: 297kcal

Carbohydrates: 31g

Protein: 21g

Fat: 3g

Sugars: 36g

Fiber: 13g

90. Roasted Strawberry Protein Smoothie

Preparation Time:	Cooking Time:	Serving
3 Minutes	12 Minutes	1

Ingredients

- 1-1/2 cups fresh strawberries, quartered
- 1/2 tbsp raw sugar
- 1/3 cup reduced-fat cottage cheese
- 1/2 cup fat-free milk
- 1 cup crushed ice
- 1 tsp chia seeds
- 6 to 8 drops of liquid stevia, optional

Directions

- Preheat oven to 425°F. In a medium bowl, combine strawberries and sugar.
- Pour the strawberries onto a parchment paper-lined baking sheet.
- Place in the oven and roast for 12 to 15 minutes until the strawberries start to release their juices but are still firm.
- Carefully pour the roasted strawberries and their juice into a blender along with cottage cheese, milk, ice and chia and blend until smooth. Enjoy!

Nutrition Info

Calories: 213kcal

Carbohydrates: 33g

Protein: 16g

Fat: 3g

Sugars: 18g

Fiber: 4g

91. Blueberry Banana Protein Smoothie

Preparation Time:	Cooking Time:	Serving
5 Minutes	0 Minutes	2

Ingredients

- ½ cup blueberries, frozen or fresh
- 1 ripe banana
- ½ cup milk
- 1 tsp vanilla extract
- 4 oz low-fat cottage cheese
- 2 tbsp chia seeds
- 1 tsp lemon zest

Directions

- Add all the ingredients to a blender, and grate in the lemon zest.
- 1 cup blueberries, frozen, 1 ripe banana, 1 cup milk, 1 tsp vanilla extract, 4oz low-fat cottage cheese,2 tbsp chia seeds, 1 tsp lemon zest. Blend. Done!

Nutrition Info

Calories: 306kcal

Carbohydrates: 41g

Protein: 27g

Fat: 14g

Sugars: 27g

Fiber: 15g

High Protein Post-Workouts

92. Raspberry Almond Chia Smoothie

Preparation Time:	**Cooking Time:**	**Serving**
5 Minutes	0 Minutes	2

Ingredients

- 2/3 cup plain Greek yogurt
- 2/3 cup almond milk
- 2/3 cup frozen raspberries
- 1/4 cup almonds, divided
- 1 tbsp. honey
- 2 tsp. chia seeds
- 1 scoop protein powder

Directions

- In a blender add all of the ingredients, reserving a few of the almonds. Blend until smooth and all ingredients are incorporated. Chop the reserved almonds to stir in if desired. Pour and enjoy.

Nutrition Info

Calories: 365kcal

Carbohydrates: 31g

Protein: 24g

Fat: 23g

Sugars: 18g

Fiber: 11g

93. Vitamin Wellness Shots

Preparation Time:	**Cooking Time:**	**Serving**
10 Minutes	0 Minutes	2

Ingredients

- 1 small orange
- 2 small lemons
- ¼ cup fresh turmeric, chopped
- ¼ cup fresh ginger, chopped
- 1/8 tsp fresh black pepper
- ¼ tsp oil (such as extra virgin, optional / to help improve turmeric absorption)

Directions

- To a juicer, add orange, lemon, turmeric, and ginger (depending on the juicer, you may need to peel the orange and lemon). Add all ingredients to the juicer or blend, until the mixture is smooth. Then strain through a clean thin dish towel, small fine mesh strainer, or nut milk bag. Just be aware that turmeric can stain.
- For Serving: Divide between serving glasses and enjoy. For maximum benefits, enjoy immediately and top with fresh cracked black pepper. Adding a little fat to improve turmeric absorption, such as olive oil!

Nutrition Info

Calories: 114kcal

Carbohydrates: 27g

Protein: 7g

Fat: 0.9g

Sugars: 27g

Fiber: 7g

94. Green Energy Juice

Preparation Time:	0Cooking Time:	Serving
10 Minutes	Minutes	2

Ingredients

- 1 bunch of kale (about 5 oz.)
- 1-inch piece of fresh ginger, peeled
- 1 large apple
- 5 celery stalks, ends trimmed
- ½ large cucumber
- A handful of fresh parsley (about 1 oz.)
- 1 scoop protein powder

Directions

- Wash and prep the vegetables. If you used a juicer, put all ingredients into it and blend well then simply pour the green juice into glasses and enjoy immediately.

Nutrition Info

Calories: 192kcal

Carbohydrates: 21g

Protein: 17g

Fat: 0.8g

Sugars: 19g

Fiber: 16g

95. Boost Detox Juice

Preparation Time:	**Cooking Time:**	**Serving**
10 Minutes	0 Minutes	2

Ingredients

- 1 carrot medium, chopped
- 1 orange peeled
- 1 green apple seeded, cored, and chopped
- 3 kale leaves
- 1 cup baby spinach
- ½ lemon peeled
- ¼ tsp ginger

Directions

- Add all the ingredients to a juicer and blend along with 2 cups of chilled water and pulse until smooth. Serve & enjoy!

Nutrition Info

Calories: 108kcal

Carbohydrates: 5g

Protein: 6g

Fat: 7.3g

Sugars: 32g

Fiber: 11g

96. Sweet Berry Juice

Preparation Time:	Cooking Time:	Serving
5 Minutes	0 Minutes	1

Ingredients

- 1 small ripe banana
- 1 cup blackberries, blueberries, raspberries, or strawberries (or use a mix)
- apple juice or mineral water, optional
- honey, to serve
- ½ scoop protein powder

Directions

- Slice the banana into your juicer or food processor and add the berries of your choice. Whizz until smooth. With the blades whirring, pour in juice or water to make the consistency you like. Toss a few extra fruits on top, drizzle with honey and serve.

Nutrition Info

Calories: 174kcal

Carbohydrates: 26g

Protein: 14g

Fat: 1g

Sugars: 18g

Fiber: 8g

97. Orange Pomegranate Juice

Preparation Time:	**Cooking Time:**	**Serving**
5 Minutes	0 Minutes	2

Ingredients

- 1 pomegranate
- 1 sprig rosemary
- 1 cinnamon stick
- ½ tsp coriander seeds
- ½ orange, sliced
- ¼ tsp orange blossom water
- 1 scoop protein powder

Directions

- Pour the pomegranate into the juicer. Add the rosemary, cinnamon stick, coriander seeds, protein powder and orange into it. Then pour through a sieve into glasses. Serve & enjoy!

Nutrition Info

Calories: 117 kcal

Carbohydrates: 14g

Protein: 16g

Fat: 0.1g

Sugars: 38g

Fiber: 16g

98. Kiwi and Kale Smoothie

Preparation Time:	**Cooking Time:**	**Serving**
5 Minutes	0 Minutes	2

Ingredients

- 1 ½ cups skim milk
- 2 cups kale stems and leaves
- 1 kiwi fruit peeled
- 1 tbsp smooth unsalted peanut butter
- 1 tsp agave nectar, honey, or maple syrup
- 1 scoop protein powder

Directions

- Blend all ingredients together. Serve!

Nutrition Info

Calories: 194kcal

Carbohydrates: 24g

Protein: 26g

Fat: 5g

Sugars: 32g

Fiber: 7g

99. Oat Cocoa Smoothie

Preparation Time:	Cooking Time:	Serving
5 Minutes	0 Minutes	1

Ingredients

- 3/4 cup skim milk
- 1 tsp vanilla extract
- ½ cup plain low-fat yogurt
- ¼ cup quick-cook oats
- 1 tbsp ground flaxseed
- 1 tsp unsweetened cocoa powder
- dash ground cinnamon or cardamom
- 1 small banana preferably frozen

Directions

- Add all ingredients to a blender. Blend on low for 20 seconds, then on high for about one minute. Serve!

Nutrition Info

Calories: 310kcal

Carbohydrates: 30g

Protein: 19g

Fat: 5g

Sugars: 28g

Fiber: 8g

100. Blueberry-Avocado Layered Smoothie

Preparation Time:	Cooking Time:	Serving
10 Minutes	0 Minutes	4

Ingredients

- 1 ripe avocado peeled and pit removed
- 1 cup low-fat plain yogurt
- Juice from ½ lime
- 1 tsp honey
- 2 scoop protein powder

Top Layer

- 1 1/3 cups wild blueberries frozen
- 1/4 cup almond butter (or smooth peanut butter)
- 1 cup low-fat plain yogurt
- 1/3 cup milk

Directions

- Blend the following: 1 ripe avocado, peeled and pit removed, 1 cup (250 ml) low-fat plain yogurt, protein powder, Juice from ½ lime and 1 tsp honey.
- Divide equally among four glasses. Set aside while making the top layer.
- Top Layer: Blend the following: 1 1/3 cup (325 ml) wild blueberries, frozen 1/4 cup (60 mL) almond butter (or smooth peanut butter) 1 cup (250 ml) low-fat plain yogurt 1/3 cup (75 ml) 1% milk. Pour into glasses, overtop avocado blend. Enjoy!

Nutrition Info

Calories: 248kcal

Carbohydrates: 16g

Protein: 21g

Fat: 19g

Sugars: 27g

Fiber: 12g

Glossary

Celcius: Measuring unit for temperature.

Cup: Measuring unit that equals 250 mL.

Defrost: The process of unfreezing frozen goods.

Dried fruits: Fruits that have their water content removed.

Farenheit: Measuring unit for temperature.

Freeze: Method of preserving food items.

Frozen: State of preserved food items.

Grams (g): Measuring unit in weight.

Half cup: Measuring unit that equals 125 mL.

Macronutrients: The essential nutrients protein, fat, and carbohydrates.

Milliliter (ml): Measuring unit in liquid form.

Ounce (oz): Measuring unit in weight.

Pounds (lbs): Measuring unit in weight.

Quarter cup: Measuring unit that equals 62.5 mL.

Raw: Food that is not cooked.

Tablespoon: Measuring unit equal to 15 mL.

Thaw: The process of unfreezing frozen goods.

References

Amino Acids in Hard-boiled eggs. (n.d.). Fitaudit. Retrieved February 12, 2023. https://fitaudit.com/food/190836/amino#:~:text=A%20branched-chain%20amino%20acid%20%28BCAA%29%20is%20a%20complex

foodrevolutionnetwork. (2019, September 6). Food Storage and Preservation: Why it Matters and How to Do it Properly. Food Revolution Network. https://foodrevolution.org/blog/food-storage-food-preservation/

Kadey, M. (2018, October 18). The 40 Best High Protein Foods. Bodybuilding. https://www.bodybuilding.com/content/ultimate-list-40-high-protein-foods.html

Kassel, G. (2022, September 30). How to Diet and Meal Prep, Bodybuilding Style. Shape. https://www.shape.com/healthy-eating/diet-tips/bodybuilding-meal-prep-ideas-nutrition#:~:text=Meal%20prep%20can%20hugely%20help%20you%20stick%20to

Liles, M. (2022, July 25). 13 Foods You Shouldn't Put In the Freezer. Allrecipes. https://www.allrecipes.com/gallery/foods-not-to-freeze/

Mayo Clinic. (2020, October 14). Water: How much should you drink every day? Mayo Clinic. https://www.mayoclinic.org/healthy-lifestyle/nutrition-and-healthy-eating/in-depth/water/art-20044256

Nalewanyj, S. (2020, August 9). 20 Common Bodybuilding Myths Debunked. Seannal. https://seannal.com/articles/training/bodybuilding-myths.php

Perling, A. (2020, May 6). Tools and Tips for Freezing Food So Nothing Goes to Waste. Wirecutter https://www.nytimes.com/wirecutter/blog/freezing-food-tips-tools/

St Pierre, B. (2020, August 24). The Ultimate Calorie, Portion, and Macro Calculator. Precision Nutrition. https://www.precisionnutrition.com/nutrition-calculator

Streit, L. (2021, November 1). What Are Macronutrients? All You Need to Know. Healthline. https://www.healthline.com/nutrition/what-are-macronutrients#food-sources

WebMD Editorial Contributors. (n.d.). What to Know About Seasonal Eating. WebMD. https://www.webmd.com/diet/what-to-know-seasonal-eating

Image References

Douglas, T. (n.d.). Roast chicken [Image]. Pexels. https://www.pexels.com/search/roast%20chicken/

Eggs [Image]. (n.d.). Pexels. https://www.pexels.com/search/eggs/

Hand [Image]. (n.d.). Pexels. https://www.pexels.com/search/carbohydrates/

Malik, K. (n.d.). Fist [Image]. Pexels. https://www.pexels.com/search/fist/

Media, K. (n.d.). Thumbs up [Image]. Pexels. https://www.pexels.com/search/tofu/

Odintsov, R. (n.d.). Protein [Image]. Pexels. https://www.pexels.com/search/protein/

Spiske, M. (n.d.). Lettuce [Image]. Pexels. https://www.pexels.com/search/lettuce/

Strawberries [Image]. (n.d.). Pexels. https://www.pexels.com/search/strawberries/

Tankilevitch, P. (n.d.). Dried fruits and nuts [Image]. Pexels. https://www.pexels.com/search/dried%20fruits%20and%20nuts/

Tankilevitch, P. (n.d.). Tofu [Image]. Pexels. https://www.pexels.com/search/tofu/

Tentil, D. (n.d.). Fish [Image]. Pexels. https://www.pexels.com/search/tofu/

Tentis, D. (n.d.). Carbohydrates [Image]. Pexels. https://www.pexels.com/search/carbohydrates/

Utsumi, R. (n.d.). Open hand [Image]. Pexels. https://www.pexels.com/search/open%20hand/

Made in the USA
Middletown, DE
27 September 2023

39545431R10077